PRESIDENTIAL SUCCESSION

*Constitution, Congress
and National Security*

PRESIDENTIAL SUCCESSION

Constitution, Congress and National Security

John C. Wohlstetter
Senior Fellow
Gold Institute for International Strategy
Discovery Institute

Published by

Gold Institute Press

Washington, DC

Printed in U.S.A.

Revised August 24th, 2024

ISBN: 979-8-9874963-3-6

A NOTE ON SOURCES

With Amendments of great historical significance, scholarly literature is an immense body of work, covering their subject—even, subsets of the overall subject—in exhaustive detail. Given its actual use in elevating one un-elected president to the Oval Office, one unelected vice-president to that office, and its serial invocation of voluntary disability by several presidents, the 25th Amendment manifestly is among the most significant subsequent additions to the U.S. Constitution.

Fortunately, there is at hand definitive scholarly work on the subject, by lawyer, scholar and educator John Feerick. His published works, spanning more than a half-century, cover the history of presidential and vice-presidential inability and the 25th Amendment, the latter from proposal through ratification, and its ultimate implementation.[1] In addition, the late Senator Birch Bayh (D-IN), prime senatorial sponsor of the 25th Amendment, penned his insider account of the deliberations in Congress leading up to its adoption, passage and ratification.[2] Attesting in detail to Feerick's special

---

[1] In 1965, Feerick published the first comprehensive study of presidential inability, *From Failing Hands*. He then published three editions covering 25th Amendment history. The first, published in 1976, was updated in the second, commemorative edition, which incorporated everything in the original volume, so that the second, 25th anniversary 1992 edition could stand on its own. The third, and final edition was published in 2014. In addition to new material, the final version substantially revised some material in the earlier editions. My 25th Amendment analysis draws from the second and third editions. Feerick also briefly returned to the topic in his 2020 memoir, *That Further Shore*. Its cover calls him—aptly—a Framer of the 25th Amendment.

[2] Bayh, Birch, *One Heartbeat Away: Presidential Disability and Succession* (Bobbs-Merrill Co., Inc., 1968).

historical and legal expertise on these matters is Sen. Bayh's foreword to the 25th anniversary commemorative edition.

Further attesting to Feerick's unique role is what he told readers of his memoir. He began researching the issue after President Eisenhower published his March 3, 1958, letter to Vice-President Nixon, stating that the president can declare his own inability, or, if unable to do so, the vice-president could make the declaration for him. By early 1963, Feerick, then in private practice at a major law firm, submitted an article on presidential inability to the Fordham Law Review. It was published in the October 1963 issue. On November 17— 5 days before JFK was killed—The New York Times published a letter on the subject from Feerick. It stated:

> *Presidents are mortal. President Garfield's shooting, President Wilson's stroke and President Eisenhower's heart attack rendered the respective President temporarily unable to exercise the powers and duties of his office. Despite this, Congress has consistently failed the American people by not acting to eliminate the possibility of a gap in the executive because of the confusion existing over the meaning of the succession provision of the Constitution.[3]*

PRESIDENTIAL SUCCESSION AND CONTINUITY OF GOVERNMENT

In the wake if the terrorist attacks or September 11, 2001, a Continuity of Government Commission (CGC) was established, consisting of present and former leaders and other recognized experts on the subject. The CGC was a joint project of the American Enterprise Institute (AEI) and the

---

[3] Feerick, John D., *That Further Shore: A Memoir of Irish Roots and American Promise*, pp. 239-240 (Fordham Univ. Press, 2020).

Brookings Institution (BI). It produced four reports before its dissolution in December 2022: (1) a May 2003 report on continuity of Congress;[4] (2) a June 2009 report on presidential succession;[5] (3) an April 2022 update report on continuity of Congress;[6] (4) a December 2022 update report on presidential succession.[7]

A NOTE ON PUNCTUATION

Cited written passages from documents and quoted oral statements differ on capitalization and use of hyphens. Each of these are presented as rendered in the original. My use of these entails use of hyphens, and use of upper-case letters for direct titular references—President X, Vice-President Y; and, excepting capitalization at the beginning of sentences, I use lowercase first letters when referring to past office-holders, *i.e.*, "the president" or "the vice-president." However, I capitalize their titles and capitalize Acting before President and Vice-President, where these are used as a particular person's title, in text that refers to events that took place when that person held that particular office. Speaker of the House is always capitalized, but I do not capitalize "President" when referring

---

[4] *Preserving Our Institutions: The Continuity of Congress*, The First Report of the Continuity of Government Commission (AEI/BI, May 2003). Hereinafter cited as CGC First Report.

[5] *Preserving Our Institutions: The Continuity of the Presidency*, The Second Report of the Continuity of Government Commission (AEI/BI, June 2009). Hereinafter cited as CGC Second Report.

[6] *The Continuity of Congress*, The Continuity of Government Commission (AEI, April 2022). Hereinafter cited as CGC Third Report.

[7] *Continuity of Government: Presidential Succession*, The Continuity of Government Commission (AEI, December 2022). Hereinafter cited as CGC Fourth Report.

to the Senate president *pro tem*. I use modern spellings for provisions of the U.S. Constitution, rather than the more aesthetically elegant archaic spellings of yesteryear.

GOLD INSTITUTE REFERENCE NOTE

References to Gold Institute for International Strategy senior fellow J. Lawrence Cunningham have no accessible citation; they were derived from conversations and emails exchanged between Cunningham and the author.

ACKNOWLEDGEMENTS

I am indebted to the support I received from both of my professional affiliations: the Gold Institute for International Strategy (GIIS) and the Discovery Institute. From them I received expert comments and suggestions toward improvement, further avenues of relevant inquiry, and encouragement at every stage of this project.

Special thanks are due Eli Gold, GIIS founder, chairman and president, for proposing this project, and repeatedly reviewing my work; J. Lawrence Cunningham, GIIS senior fellow, for lending his expertise derived from 20 years in the Secret Service, including developing plans and procedures for protecting presidents at home and abroad, and for visiting foreign dignitaries (the latter including a Pope, and several heads of state); and Saul Montes-Bradley II, GIIS vice-president, communications, who reviewed my manuscript and oversaw its final preparation for publication.

Special thanks also to Larry Cunningham and Adam Lovinger (also a GIIS senior fellow) for taking the time to review and comments on the entire book, and for their testimonials on my behalf.

Without their assistance this project would not resemble the final product. Needless to say, for errors of commission and omission, and any other shortcomings, I bear and thus fully accept sole responsibility.

TABLE OF CONTENTS

PROLOGUE

A LEADERSHIP CRISIS
IN PARLOUS TIMES

A Scenario Published in June 2009

On the night of the President's annual State of the Union address, a commercial jet piloted by a clandestine terrorist takes off from Reagan National Airport, immediately banks away from its scheduled flight path and heads straight for the Capitol. It covers the three miles in minutes, before any weapon that can destroy the plane can be activated and fired. The Capitol roof is demolished, and there are clearly hundreds dead, and hundreds more wounded. Somehow, the president, though badly injured, is rescued, and he appears a couple of days later on nationwide television to report on steps he intends to take in response to the attacks:

> *Even the august setting of the Oval Office, perfect lighting and professional makeup cannot hide the fact that the President is not well. His frequent pauses, confusion over basic facts, and general demeanor frighten rather than reassure the American public.*

This scenario was presented in the June 2009 CGC Second Report.[8]

The Biden presidency has presented Americans with a protracted crisis: a president clearly exhibiting increasing signs of physical deterioration and mental cognitive decline, and a vice-president widely viewed as manifestly unfit to ascend to the presidency.[i]

---

[8] CGC Second Report, note 5 *supra.*, p. 21.

These realities are recognized by a broad cross-section of the voting public, to say nothing of key leaders abroad. Florida Governor Ron De Santis, openly proclaimed[ii] in July 2022:

> *So here's the thing – I thought Biden picking her at first was like the worst decision ever because she's not great. But she's like the best impeachment insurance and 25th amendment insurance anyone could have. Because as bad as Biden is, even though he can barely read the teleprompter, and as much as people disapprove of him, nobody wants Harris, and so they'd much rather stick with Biden floundering around than actually turn the wheels of power over to somebody that clearly is in over her head.*

This July 22, 2021, video and interview[iii], featuring Dr. Ronny Jackson, formerly White House physician to presidents Obama and Trump, now a Republican member of the House of Representatives, captures in a medical nutshell what Governor DeSantis described.

Adding fuel to the fire is that during Donald Trump's first year in office, Democrats called for the president to resign for alleged inability to meet the mental demands of the presidency. On January 16, 2018, Jackson, in response to persistent assertions that President Trump was not of sound mind, announced[iv] that the president had taken the Montreal Cognitive Assessment test[v] and aced it, answering all 30 questions correctly.

On July 27, 2021, 54 Republican members of Congress (including Ronny Jackson) called upon[vi] the president to take a cognitive test and disclose the results to the public. President Biden's February 8, 2024, assertion[vii] that he was of sound mind did not resonate with the public. On February 12, Jackson stated[viii] that he had observed a steep decline in President Biden's mental acuity compared to his two terms as vice-president, when Jackson frequently had interactions with Biden. Jackson said: "And the 25th Amendment, if you look at section 4, was written for exactly what we're seeing right now." On Feb. 8, Senator Rick Scott (R-FL) called[ix] for the president to resign, based upon special counsel Robert Hur's report that the president had "a poor memory"; Scott said such a person "[should not] be commander-in-chief of our armed forces.

These assessments are not confined[x] to Republicans nor, as to age, to Biden. An ABC poll of nationwide voter attitudes show that, after Biden's February 8 appearance:

(1) 86 percent, including 73 percent of Democrats, think President Biden is too old to run again—up 12 points from September 2023;
(2) 61 percent, including 35 percent of Republicans, think former president Trump is too old to run again—up 13 points from September 2023;
(3) 59 percent think both Biden and Trump are too old to run again.

A February 8, 2024, NBC News poll asked[xi] voters whether President Biden and former president Trump "[had the] necessary physical and mental health to be president": 76 percent had "major or moderate concerns" as to Biden, and 48 percent felt the same as to Trump.

A February 8, 2024 NBC report detailed[xii] concerns of Democrats as to Biden's cognitive functions, and noted rebuttals from the president's supporters:

Special counsel Robert Hur's portrait of a man who couldn't remember when he served as Barack Obama's vice president, or the year when his beloved son Beau died, dealt a blow to Biden's argument that he is still sharp and fit enough to serve another four-year term.

Trump at this writing has yet to show any evidence of lack of mental capacity, but a September 13, 2023, Quinnipiac University poll found[xiii] that by a 61 to 34 percent margin voters think that there should be an age cap for presidential candidates.

A telling signal for President Biden's cognitive decline is that he declined an invitation to be interviewed for 20 to 25 minutes during the Super Bowl telecast; Clinton political strategist James Carville noted[xiv] that this shows Biden's staff lacks confidence in his ability to do such a live interview. The February 11, 2024, Super Bowl LVIII audience reached[xv] 123.4 million; this was more than thrice the audience for President Biden's March 7, 2024, State of the Union address, which reached[xvi] 38.2 million viewers.

President Biden's performance in his June 27 debate with former president Trump engendered near universal shock. Early in the debate Biden had an episode of slurred speech, and then a brain freeze. Finally, there was the spectacle of First Lady Jill Biden escorting her clearly physically frail husband off the debate stage. CNN's chief national correspondent, John King stated that the Democrats, after a "game changing" debate, are in "a deep, a wide and a very aggressive panic" over Biden's disastrous performance. He added that among the options party insiders are considering is to visit the president at the White House and ask him to step down, or to have "prominent" Democrats call publicly for his resignation. The next day saw the New York Times editorial board—literally the Bible for many influential Democrats— call upon the president to step down; other major newspapers followed suit. A Harvard CAPS/Harris poll taken the weekend after the debate found that 66 percent of registered voters doubt Biden's mental fitness, up 12 points since May; 74 percent think he is too old, up 11 points since May; and 54 percent think he has gotten worse as president, up 5 points since May.

ORGANIZATION OF THE WORK

Part I
Covers assassination, because the complex events surrounding assassination raise certain distinct issues not present in cases of ordinary disability, whether voluntary or involuntary. Assassination is also potentially tectonic in its impact, striking a blow against the very foundation of government by law and public consent.

Included in this section are cases where near-misses against presidents or presidential candidates (plus one targeting a Supreme Court justice) altered the course of history. Also included is one assassination whose impact was arguably comparable to successful presidential assassinations: the murder of Senator Robert F. Kennedy in 1968, thus denying him the presidency he might well have won.

Part II
Covers presidential disability from George Washington through Dwight Eisenhower (1789-1960), and the growing concern that something had to be done before a crisis arose that could not be managed lawfully.

Part III
Covers the genesis, debate, adoption, and ratification of the 25th Amendment (1961-1967).

Part IV
Covers implementation of section 1 (automatic vice-presidential succession), section 2 (nomination and confirmation of a new vice-president), and section 3 (voluntary presidential disability and the role of the vice-president as Acting President) (1973-2024).

Part V
Covers section 4 of the 25th Amendment (involuntary presidential disability), to date unused, via six presidential disability scenarios.

Part VI
Covers protection of presidents, vice-presidents, their families, presidential candidates, foreign dignitaries, and major special events.

Part VII
Covers unresolved Constitutional and statutory issues, including (a) the interpretation of language amounting to an emergency clause within the language of section 4; and (b) the possible revival of a statutory power to call a special election, in event that all successors per the 25th Amendment and the extant 1947 presidential succession law are killed.

Part VIII
Covers continuity of government after mass-casualty events, and their resulting interplay among the three branches of the federal government.

Part IX

Offers the author's own conclusions and recommendations.

PREFATORY HISTORICAL NOTE

PRESIDENTIAL/VICE PRESIDENTIAL VACANCIES

Excluding the incomplete Biden term, of 45 presidents, 9 failed to complete their term: 8 died in office (4 by assassination, 4 by natural causes), and one resigned. Of 48 prior vice-presidents, 18 failed to complete their term; 9 ascended by succession to the presidency; 7 died in office; and 2 resigned their office. The vice-presidency was vacant for 37-3/4 years—21 percent of the 179 years prior to the effective ratification date of the 25th Amendment which provided formal procedures for filling vice-presidential vacancies.[9]

During those 179 years for more than 8 of the 37-3/4 years (22 percent) without a sitting vice-president, presidential succession would have devolved to a member of Congress (Senate president pro tem,[10] *or Speaker of the House) from the opposing political party.*[11]

---

[9] Feerick, John D., *The Twenty-Fifth Amendment: Its Complete History and Applications*, Appendices D & E, pp. 254-257 (25th Anny. Ed., Ford. Univ. Press, 1992). For vice-presidents, see Wikipedia list (https://en.wikipedia.org/wiki/List_of_vice_presidents_of_the_United_States)

[10] The offices of vice-president, Speaker of the House and president *pro tem* (Latin abbreviation of *tempore*, meaning temporary) of the Senate were creations of the U.S. Constitution. *See* Art. I, sec. 2 (Speaker); Art. I, sec. 3 (Senate president *pro tem*); and Art. II, sec. 1 (vice-president).

[11] *The Twenty-Firth Amendment*, 25th Anny. ed., note 9 *supra*, p. 237. Most notable of the instances when presidents faced opposition leaders in Congress came during the partial-term presidencies of John Tyler, Millard Fillmore and Harry Truman—the Senate president *pro tem* during the Tyler and Fillmore presidencies, and the Speaker of the House during Truman's first, partial, term. During the Clinton, Bush Jr., Obama, Trump and Biden presidencies (1993-2022), the House was **controlled** by the opposition party for a total of 20 years through end-2022. In January 2023 the Republicans took the House, but with

a diminishing razor-thin margin due to candidate retirements and resignations; it is unclear if Republicans will control the House for the remainder of President Biden's term. During the same period, the opposition party **controlled** the Senate for 9-2/3 years—the fractional year coming when in early 2001, Vermont GOP senator James Jeffords switched parties. (The House and Senate actually meet 2 to 2-1/2 weeks before each quadrennial Presidential term begins; when January 3 falls on a weekend, Congress meets on a following weekday. For reader convenience these days are not tallied.)

PART I:
THE ASSASSIN'S VETO (1865-1981)

Abraham Lincoln 1865
Last Casualty of the Civil War.

During the Civil War the Pinkerton Detective Agency,[xvii] founded in 1850, provided security for the new president from 1861. But after John Wilkes Booth, a Confederate sympathizer adamantly opposed to the abolition of slavery, murdered the president almost universally regarded as America's greatest, a Treasury Department official, William Wood, was assigned to investigate the killing. Booth had enlisted[xviii] ten co-conspirators.[12] The Secret Service was established July 5, 1865, with Wood as its first chief, as part of the Treasury

---

[12] Besides Booth, they were: Samuel Arnold, a Confederate veteran; George A. Atzerodt, a carriage painter and footman; David E. Herold, a friend of Atzerodt's; Dr. Samuel A. Mudd, who set Booth's broken leg, aiding his escape; Michael O'Laughlen, a Confederate veteran; Lewis Powell, a confederate veteran; Edman "Ned" Spangler, a stagehand and carpenter at Ford's Theatre; John Harrison Surratt, Jr., a Confederate spy; Mary E. Surratt, who owned a boardinghouse used by several of the conspirators. After Booth's death, eight conspirators were tried in 1866, of whom four were **hanged**: Powell, who seriously wounded the secretary of state, William Seward; Herold, who guided Powell to Seward's residence and aided Booth's escape; Atzerodt, who was tasked with assassinating Vice-President Andrew Johnson, but abandoned his mission and got drunk; and Mary Surratt, who became the first woman executed by the U.S. government. The other four, tried in 1866, received jail sentences; one of the jailed co-conspirators, O'Laughlen, died in jail in 1867. The ninth co-conspirator, John Surratt, fled the country in 1865, was caught and extradited in 1867, and was tried that year. His trial ended in a hung jury. In 1869, Andrew Johnson pardoned Arnold, Mudd and Spangler, and allowed Mary Surratt's remains to be delivered to her daughter, Anna, for burial in the family plot. Only those who were executed, plus John Surratt, knew of the impromptu murder plot, after the original plan of kidnapping was abandoned. Mary Surratt's execution was controversial, for want of evidence that she knew of the final plan.

Department. However, it was originally tasked with removing counterfeit paper currency from circulation. *Treasury then estimated that from one-third to one-half the paper currency in circulation was counterfeit.*[13]

Lincoln became the first-ever president to make constructive use of his vice-president, frequently asking Hannibal Hamlin's advice; but Hamlin was replaced on the 1864 ticket by Democrat Andrew Johnson—ironically, like Booth, a Confederate sympathizer. Delegates at the GOP convention believed that the Civil War's imminent end required at the national level a figure who might encourage reconciliation. Booth was the spearpoint of a conspiracy, whose members planned to kidnap Lincoln on March 17. After that plan fell through, and with their number reduced to four, on April 14 they implemented a hastily contrived plan to kill Lincoln, Johnson and secretary of state William Seward. Seward was seriously injured; Johnson, upon learning this, fled his residence and thus escaped harm.[14]

Booth arrived at Ford's Theater at 10:15 PM, as the third act of the play, an English drawing room comedy, *Our American Cousin*, began. He worked his way upstairs, entered the president's box, and positioned himself behind the president. He waited until scene 2, when he knew that there was a line that always made audiences laugh. He fired his pistol during the laughter, muffling the sound of the shot. Shouting his

---

[13] Leonnig, Carol, *Zero Fail: The Rise and Fall of the Secret Service* (Random House, 2021), pp. 9-14.

[14] Feerick, John D., *From Failing Hands: The Story of Presidential Succession* (Fordham Univ. Press, 1965), pp. 107-112.

infamous line, *"Sic semper tyrannis!"* ("Ever thus to tyrants!"), he leaped onto the stage, pulled a knife and ran for the exit.[15] Booth was unique among presidential assassins in American history. Far from the deranged loner exiled from polite society, he was a celebrated actor, whose acclaim was matched only by his brother Edwin, known as the Prince of Players. In the 1860s, John Wilkes Booth was making between $25,000 and $30,000 annually, comparable[xix] to President Lincoln's $25,000 salary. The Booth theatrical family was the most celebrated in early America. Their father, Junius Booth, was the most celebrated of his generation. Their paternal grandfather, also named John Wilkes Booth, had been a prominent leader of parliamentary opposition to none other than King George III.[16]

Booth's family-bred penchant for opposing rulers found fertile soil in southern Maryland, and in Baltimore, his place of residence during the war years; *in 1860 a grand total of 12 voters in Maryland's five southernmost counties cast their ballot for Lincoln.*[17] Booth attended Lincoln's March 4, 1865 inauguration at which Lincoln closed[xx] his address with words that would resonate with most Americans and haunt his killer:

---

[15] Kauffman, Michael W., *American Brutus: John Wilkes Booth and the Lincoln Conspiracies* (Random House, 2005), pp. 4-10. The reliable laugh line was spoken by the lead character, Asa Trenchard, the American rustic cousin who went to England to claim his inheritance, to an English lady who had chastised him for proposing marriage to her daughter. His answer was: *"Don't know the manner of English society, eh? Well, I guess I know enough to turn you inside out, old gal, you sockdologizing [sic] old mantrap."* It is from English playwright Tom Taylor's *Our American Cousin*, p. 54 (Independent Pub., May 29, 2020).

[16] *Id.,* pp. 84-85.

[17] *Id.,* p. 144.

With malice toward none; with charity for all; with firmness in the right, as God gives us to see the right, let us strive on to finish the work we are in; to bind up the nation's wounds; to care for him who shall have borne the battle, and for his widow, and his orphan ~ to do all which may achieve and cherish a just and lasting peace among ourselves and with all nations.

Afterwards, Booth told friends: "What an excellent chance I had to kill the president, if I had wished, on Inauguration Day! I was on the stand, as close to him nearly as I am to you." When one friend scorned him— "You're crazy, John. What good would that do?" Tellingly, Booth said: "I could live in history."[18] He later told friends in Philadelphia, "You will hear from me in Washington. I am going to make a big hit."[19] The day of reckoning was April 11, two days after U.S. Grant accepted the Confederate Army surrender by Robert E. Lee at Appomattox, and three days before Good Friday at Ford's Theatre. Booth attended a speech in which the president laid out his plans for postwar reconstruction, and which he stated his support for limited voting rights for African Americans. Booth remarked: "That means n———r citizenship. Now, by God, I'll put him through."[20]

But in doing so, would-be avenging angel Booth saw the exact opposite public reaction, across the political spectrum, north and south: the unifying reconstruction that Lincoln's Inaugural and his April 11 speech proposed.[21] Newspapers

---

[18] *Id.*, p. 205.

[19] *Id.*

[20] *Id.*, p. 210

[21] *Id., p. 237.*

that had often savaged the president during the conflict changed sides: The Washington *Evening Star* said: "History has on its record no suicidal act so terrible as that committed by the conquered South yesterday." The Richmond *Whig* called it "the most appalling, the most deplorable calamity which has ever befallen the people of the United States."[22] Booth biographer Michael Kauffman titled his book *American Brutus* because like Julius Caesar's Brutus, his act made his victim a martyr.[23]

Booth's last 12 days were spent on the run. Given the advantage of surprise, and having positioned his horse near a rear exit, Booth had a huge head start, escaping the city before the city was barricaded to facilitate hunting down co-conspirators. Once the pursuit got organized, including telegraph and steamboat, in a single day the posse covered the distance from downtown Washington to the Port Conway ferry that would take Booth from Maryland into Virginia; it had taken the injured Booth ten days to reach the ferry.[24]

Presidents know they are targets. But Lincoln went one step further. Lincoln biographer Harold Holzer recounts how the president, asleep in the White House, was beset by a premonition that came upon him in a dream. Awoken by sounds of people sobbing, he went downstairs to the East Room, where he saw a catafalque. He asked a soldier "Who is dead in the White House?" The soldier answered: "The president. He was killed by an assassin." Lincoln couldn't get

---

[22] *Id.*, p. 271.

[23] *Id.*, p. 398.

[24] Swanson, James L., *Manhunt: The 12-day Chase for Lincoln's Killer* (HarperCollins, 2007), p. 289.

back to sleep.[25] Indeed, in 1862 a bullet fired by either a would-be assassin or a sentry unaware of at whom he was shooting, passed through Lincoln's stovepipe hat as he rode from the White House towards his summer home outside the city. Lincoln dismissed the shooter as "a disloyal bushwhacker." His aide, Ward Hill Lemon, persuaded Lincoln to stop riding alone. Lincoln responded that "Oh, assassination of public officers is not an American crime."[26]

In a bizarre post-death twist, a protracted dispute erupted between the Lincoln family and state authorities, as to where he would be laid to rest. A team of counterfeiters whose members had done jail time due to having been caught by the Secret Service, concocted a scheme to steal Lincoln's body and hold it for ransom. In the end, it failed, but Lincoln's coffin was moved several times, before reaching its final resting place, on September 26, 1901.[27]

James Garfield 1881: Triple Succession Vacancy.

On the morning of July 2, Garfield, a mere 124 days into his term—triple Lincoln's 41 days into his second term—was shot twice as he prepared to board a train at Washington, D.C.'s Union Station. One bullet grazed his arm; the other struck him in the back. The assassin, Charles Guiteau, an unsuccessful office-seeker, declared upon his immediate

---

[25] Holzer, Harold, *President Lincoln Assassinated!!: The Firsthand Story of the Murder, Manhunt, Trial and Mourning* (Library of America special publication, 2014), p. xv.

[26] *Id.*, p. xvii. Assassinating a president did not become a federal crime until after the assassination of JFK. See Part III.

[27] Craughwell, Thomas J., *Stealing Lincoln's Body* (Belknap Press, 2007).

apprehension: "I did it and will go to jail for it. I am a Stalwart, and Arthur will be president."[28]

The Republican Party was deeply split into two factions over the issue of civil service reform. The Stalwarts, who included Garfield's assassin, supported continuance of federal civil service patronage; Garfield's faction, the Half-Breeds, supported civil service reform. Two letters were found in Guiteau's pockets: one addressed to the White House, which stated: "The president's tragic death was a sad necessity, but it will again unite the Republican party and save the republic.... I had no ill-will toward the president.... His death was a political necessity." The other was addressed to Vice-President Chester Arthur and included Guiteau's recommendations for Cabinet appointees.[29]

Ironically, while Guiteau's second bullet, lodged near Garfield's spine, was officially the cause of death, Garfield likely would have lived had mid-19th century advances in

---

[28] *Failing Hands*, note 14 *supra*, p. 118. The Stalwart faction of the GOP had supported Ulysses S. Grant for the 1880 nomination to what would have been his third term; Guiteau knew that Vice-President Chester Arthur was also a Stalwart. There had been an internal struggle within the GOP over patronage reform. *Id.*, p. 120. Confounding expectations—including Guiteau's—Arthur adopted Garfield's civil service reform program and signed the Pendleton Civil Service Act in 1883. Millard, Candice, *Destiny of the Republic: A Tale of Madness, Medicine, and the Murder of a President*, p. 250 (Doubleday, 2011).

[29] *Id.*, p. 121.

medical sanitation been applied by his doctors.[30] The first doctor to treat Garfield, as he lay on the Union Station platform, a veritable germ-factory setting, made things far worse by inserting his unwashed fingers into Garfield's back to try to find the bullet; he caused a hemorrhage that became a severe infection.[31] Alexander Graham Bell developed an "induction balance" device in a race against the clock, that was used to finally locate the bullet.[32] But by the time Bell's device proved successful, Garfield, gravely weakened, was beyond saving.[33]

During his 80 days lingering before the president succumbed to blood poisoning caused by the fatal bullet, part of the time there were vacancies in both the offices of Senate president *pro tem* and Speaker of the House. After the vice-president, only these could be elevated to the presidency, per the then-existing Constitutional and statutory provisions.[34]

Chester Arthur, in his 1881 message to Congress, raised numerous succession issues as to presidential disability and apportionment of power between a disabled president and the

---

[30] *Destiny of the Republic*, note 28 *supra*, pp. 14-17. British surgeon Joseph Lister had developed a theory of *antisepsis*—killing germs during surgery. By the last quarter of the 19th century Lister's view had been adopted widely in Europe. Alas, it was not so in the U.S. Exposing open wounds to air, and soaking them in warm water were preferred methods of treatment. Garfield's doctors followed the majority U.S. view, to Garfield's detriment.

[31] *Id.*, p. 138.

[32] *Id.*, pp. 199-200.

[33] *Id.* pp. 257-58.

[34] *From Failing Hands*, note 14 *supra*, pp. 130-31.

vice-president. Many were resolved by the 1967 ratification of the 25th Amendment. But some issues pertaining to the involuntary disability of the president under section 4 remain unresolved. Feerick writes of Arthur's long list that there has been "no more complete statement of this manifold problem."[35]

William McKinley 1901:
The Secret Service Fails its First Test.

In his history of the McKinley assassination, author Scott Miller cites an anti-McKinley New York Journal editorial (owned by "yellow journalism"[xxi] magnate William Randolph Hearst), months before the September 6 assassination, that said: "If bad men and bad institutions can only be get rid of by killing, then the killing must be done."[36]

On the fateful day, a young anarchist, Leon Czolgosz, inspired by the assassination of Italian monarch Umberto I, and a profoundly frustrated witness to the overt plutocratic excesses of the Gilded Age, went to an event for the president at the Pan-American Exposition of 1901. Watching spectators' line up to greet the president, a prominent Buffalo attorney quipped, referencing the vice-president: "It would be Roosevelt's luck to have McKinley shot today."[37] Czolgosz waited his turn, pulled a pistol from his hip pocket, and fired. *Incredibly, none of the Secret Service agents, police and soldiers*

---

[35] *Id.*, pp. 138-39. The full list of questions raised by Arthur, and their status at present, is presented in Appendix I

[36] Miller, Scott, *The President and the Assassin: McKinley, Terror and Empire at the Dawn of the American Century* (Random House Trade Paperbacks, 2011), p. 5.

[37] *Id., p. 8.*

scrutinizing the spectators in line as they approached the front asked Czolgosz to pull his right hand out of his pocket.[38]

McKinley had been remarkably accessible during the campaign, having conducted in 1896 the nation's first "Front Porch" campaign: Between June 19 and November 2, 750,000 visitors in 300 delegations from 30 states visited, with nary a Secret Service agent present.[39] Eerily prefiguring the 2020 campaign, while McKinley remained at home, Democrat nominee William Jennings Bryan, a charismatic populist, traveled around the country, covering 18,000 miles by rail, giving 600 speeches in 27 states, reaching 5 million people. He once gave 36 speeches in a single day.[40] Bryan had campaigned on backing currency with inflationary bimetallism—in his "cross of gold" convention address: "You shall not press down upon the brow of labor this crown of thorns; you shall not crucify mankind on a cross of gold."[41] His charisma, however, did not prevail on Election Day.

---

[38] *Id.*, p. 10. There was an X-ray machine at the Exposition, but no one on the site who knew how to operate it; Thomas Edison knew, but he was not at the grounds that day. Oliver, Willard M. & Marion, Nancy E., *Killing the President: Assassinations, Attempts, and Rumored Attempts on U.S. Commanders-in-Chief* (Praeger, 2010), p. 64. Theodore Roosevelt was climbing Mt. Marcy, the state's highest peak, and was sworn in 12 hours after McKinley died. *Id.*, p. 66.

[39] *The President and the Assassin*, note 36 *supra*, p. 13.

[40] *Id.*, pp. 25-26.

[41] *Id.*, p. 25.

John F. Kennedy 1963:
Presidential Luck Runs Out.

America had gone just over 62 years without a president being killed in office. The multiple illnesses of Eisenhower had failed to generate consensus to address presidential succession.[42] LBJ went 14 months after his accession before, upon his 1965 inauguration, America again had a vice-president. He thus resolved to fix the problem once and for all. The result, which fixed most, but not all problems, was the 1967 ratification of the 25th Amendment.[43]

RFK 1968:
An Assassin Tilts the U.S. Presidential Election.

LBJ's March 31, 1968, announcement that he would not seek re-election triggered a scramble for the nomination. On June 5, Sen. Robert F. Kennedy, having entered the race shortly after LBJ withdrew, won the California primary, and was headed for likely nomination at the Democratic Convention in August. Vice-President Humphrey, his chief rival, was saddled with the albatross of the unpopular Vietnam War and lacked RFK's personal and familial charisma. RFK was shot right after his California primary celebration.[44] RFK might

---

[42] The ultimately unsuccessful effort to revise presidential succession laws is covered in Part II. The JFK/LBJ years are covered in Part III. Additional material on the events of November 22, 1963, is covered in Part VI.

[43] The 25th Amendment is covered in detail in Part III.

[44] There are countless books purporting to prove conspiracies surrounding the JFK and RFK assassinations. Some implicate famous figures; some allege multiple shooters; others allege shadow domestic governments or blame foreign governments. Sifting through these is way beyond the timeframe of the

well have defeated Richard Nixon, who was equally lacking as was Humphrey in charisma. Thus did an assassin arguably decide the 1968 presidential contest.

NEAR MISSES

Andrew Jackson (1835).

On January 30, 1835, in the first-ever attempt on a president's life, an ambidextrous would-be assassin, later judged insane, tried to shoot Jackson with two pistols while he attended funeral services in the Capitol. Fortunately, both of his pistols misfired.[45]

Theodore Roosevelt 1912:
Ex-President Targeted.

TR ran as a third-party candidate, seeking to unseat his presidential successor, William Howard Taft. On October 4, John Schrank, a tavern-keeper who harbored insane delusions

---

author, who aims to inform public discussion of the current, urgent leadership crisis.

[45] *Failing Hands*, note 14 *supra*, p. 86. Richard Lawrence became mentally unstable in 1832, believing that the U.S. government would pay his return to his native England, and that only Andrew Jackson's opposition to creating a national bank stood in his way; he believed that if Martin van Buren became president, he would get his money, return home, and be recognized there as Richard III. *Killing the President*, note 38 *supra*, p. 5. The role of insanity in prosecuting assassins was brought to the fore after the assassination attempt on President Reagan, covered later in this section. In 1835 there had been no court cases adjudicating defense insanity claims. For more on the insanity defense, see the section below, on President Reagan.

that TR had engineered the killing of McKinley, shot TR in the chest; the bullet was deflected by TR's metal eyeglass case and a folded copy of his 100-page speech.[46]

Franklin D. Roosevelt 1933:
Assassin's Miss Kills Chicago's Mayor.

Guiseppe Zangara earned the dubious distinction of being the first assassin to fire shots and miss, killing Mayor Anton Cermak. Zangara, tormented by physical illness, and resentful of his poverty, attempted to kill FDR, then president-elect, on February 15, 1933, 17 days before FDR's inauguration. Zangara was executed on March 20, 33 days after his arrest on the spot.[47]

Harry Truman 1947 and 1951:
Two Failed Attempts.

---

[46] *Killing the President*, note 38 *supra*, pp. 73-81. Schrank was furious that TR was seeking a third term, which went beyond George Washington's two-term precedent. While TR did not think Secret Service protection would be effective, he also said: "I do not believe there is any danger of such an assault." The bullet was also deflected by TR's right ribcage, and his overall musculature. Thus, it did not puncture his lung, and stopped one-inch from his heart. Absent the precise deflection angle the bullet would have struck his heart and aorta, in which event TR would have died in less than 60 seconds. *Id.* Ironically, as president, TR had two narrow escapes: in his first term an intruder was caught with a firearm outside the White House; in his second, an intruder, carrying a sharp blade up his sleeve, made it into the Oval Office. *Id.*, p. 75.

[47] Picchi, Blaise, *The Five Weeks of Giuseppe Zangara: The Man Who Would Assassinate FDR* (Academy Chicago Publishers, 1998). Zangara told police in Miami that he had considered killing President Hoover, but decided that Washington, D.C. was too cold. His desire to kill was directed against the presidency itself, and not the person in office. *Id.*, p. 79.

HST's presidency was tumultuous and highly consequential; he also endured a dubious first: the first president to survive *confirmed* multiple attempts[xxii] on his life.[48] In 1947 a letter bomb was mailed to the White House, where it was successfully disarmed.[49] On November 1, 1950 Puerto Rican nationalists seeking to advance the cause of independence for the island attempted to kill Truman when he and his wife were in residence at Blair House, while the White House underwent a major renovation. Leslie Coffelt, one of the Secret Service agents with Truman's protective detail, was killed, as was one of the terrorists. The surviving terrorist, Oscar Colazzo, was sentenced to death, but in 1952 Truman commuted his sentence to life, and in 1979 President Carter pardoned him. Ironically, Truman had been a strong supporter of granting Puerto Rico full Commonwealth status, had named the first native Puerto Rican governor of the island, and had made islanders eligible to receive Social Security benefits. In 1952 the island became a Commonwealth.[50]

---

[48] An unconfirmed possible assassination attempt on a president is covered in Part I, in the section on Abraham Lincoln. Two possible attempts when TR was president, neither fully confirmed, took place inside the White House, one during each presidential term. See fn. 46.

[49] The 1947 attempt by letter bomb was by the Stern Gang, a fringe Jewish terror group that was at odds with the Jewish Agency; had they succeeded, Truman would not have been around to recognize Israel upon its declaring independence on May 14, 1948. As Truman was alone among top U.S. leaders to support Israel's creation, history would have been dramatically altered. *Killing the President*, note 38 *supra*, pp. 111-12.

[50] The gun battle saw 27 rounds fired in two minutes. Had the terrorists seen the president's schedule, and waited a half hour, they may well have gotten a clear shot at the president. McCullough, David, *Truman*, pp. 808-813 (Simon & Schuster, 1992). The assassins would have faced at least 20 agents to reach Truman inside. *Killing the President*, note 38 *supra*, p. 111.

Truman's brush with death had long-term consequences. No longer did he walk across the street to the White House, often chatting with passers-by. The presidential limousine was made bullet-proof; Truman said the car could "turn a grenade" and the floor could "stop a land mine."[51]

Gerald Ford 1975:
Two Lucky Escapes.

In 1975 two would-be assassins tried to shoot President Ford. One, Lynette "Squeaky" Fromme, a member of the Charles Manson "family"[xxiii] albeit not implicated in any of the cult's murders, tried to shoot Ford with a .45 caliber handgun at point-blank range. She pulled the trigger, but a Secret Service agent prevented the gun from firing. Convicted of attempted murder, and sentenced to life, she was paroled in 2009.[52] (Ironically, as a child, Fromme had been part of a dance group that appeared on the Lawrence Welk Show[xxiv] and at the White House.[53])

Just 17 days later, the second would-be assassin, Sara Jane Moore, fired her .30 caliber handgun at a 40-foot range, narrowly missing the president; her second attempt was deflected by an alert bystander before she could fire. Incredibly, Moore *had been arrested the day before for illegal possession of a handgun but was immediately released.*[54]

---

[51] *Truman*, note 50 supra, p. 813. What Truman said was not literally true.

[52] *Killing the President*, note 38 *supra*, pp. 136-38.

[53] *Id.*

[54] *Id.*, pp. 140-43. The authorities did not arrest Moore because she had once been an FBI informant.

Ronald Reagan 1981
Secret Service Saves the Day

Ronald Reagan had an even closer call, having actually been shot. The would-be assassin, John Hinckley, had become obsessed with the idea of killing a president after watching actor Robert DeNiro in *Taxi Driver*, a 1976 film in which DeNiro's character, a psychotic veteran who drifts into New York's seedy nightlife scene, considers assassinating a presidential candidate to impress an underage prostitute, played by actress Jodie Foster. Hinckley had developed a crush on her, even writing her letters seeking her affections, only to encounter repeated rejection. He decided that he could impress her sufficiently if he assassinated a president.[55] His first effort began when he flew to Texas to buy two guns. He then returned to Washington, D.C. and rented a hotel room three blocks from the White House. In October 1980 he stalked Carter to Dayton, Ohio and Nashville, Tennessee. Abandoning his effort, he went to the Nashville airport, where airport security detected his guns. Arrested for illegal possession of a firearm, he was fined $62.50.[56]

Hinckley resumed his quest after Ronald Reagan's election. Learning that the president would give a speech to union supporters at the Washington Hilton Hotel on the afternoon

---

[55] Wilber, Del Quentin, *Rawhide Down: The Near Assassination of Ronald Reagan*, pp. 37-38 (Henry Holt & Co., 2011). "Rawhide" was President Reagan's Secret Service code name.

[56] *Id.*, pp. 70-71.

of March 30, Hinckley stood in a crowd and rapidly fired six shots from his .22 revolver as Reagan exited the hotel's rear entrance. One bullet ricocheted off the presidential limousine and struck the president; another gravely wounded press secretary James Brady; one bullet each struck Secret Service agent Timothy McCarthy and D.C. police officer Thomas Delahanty.[57]

Reagan's survival was miraculous. The bullet was a "Devastator" designed to explode upon impact. Instead, it had fragmented, and entered his lung—one inch from his heart. Jerry Parr, the Secret Service agent who had pushed Reagan into the presidential limo and rolled on top of him, noticed foamy blood on Reagan's lips, indicating a punctured lung. The car was headed back to the White House, the originally preferred destination for reasons of security, in case other assassins were at large. Parr immediately ordered the driver to head for nearby George Washington University Hospital. His decision saved Reagan's life.[58]

Put on trial for his crimes, Hinckley won an acquittal by pleading insanity, which sparked public outrage and caused many states to narrow the scope of insanity defense laws.[59] Problems with these cases arise because of divergence between legal and medical concepts of insanity. The first

---

[57] Id., 77-87.

[58] *Id.*, 88-101. Reagan had lost nearly half his blood. *Zero Fail*, note 13 *supra*, p. 132. Most of the doctors and nurses attending him thought Reagan would die. See fn. 221, *infra*.

[59] Bonnie, Richard J., Jeffries, Jr., John C., and Low, Peter W., *A Case Study in the Insanity Defense: The Trial of John W. Hinckley, Jr.* (Foundation Press, 4th ed., 2021).

instance of insanity, under the term "madness," appears in 12th century English criminal law, not as a defense to conviction at trial, but in the form of discretionary royal pardon. Fast forward to 1505, when the first case of acquittal at a criminal trial was recorded. The first formal definition of legal insanity came in an 1843 English case. Daniel M'Naghten, suffering from extreme paranoia, believing that prime minister Sir Robert Peel was persecuting him, shot and killed Edward Drummond, Peel's secretary, whom he mistakenly believed was Peel.[60]

The "Rule in M'Naghten's Case" was propounded by the judge via his instructions to the jury:

> *[W]hether ... at the time the act was committed [defendant] had that competent use of his understanding as that he knew what he was doing, by the very act itself, a wicked and a wrong thing... But if... you think the prisoner capable of distinguishing between right and wrong, then he was a responsible agent...*[61]

In essence, the Rule turns on two concepts: (1) Did the defendant know the "nature and quality" of his act; and (2) Did the defendant know that the act is wrong.[62] One might illustrate this with a simple example: Did the defendant know he was shooting a person, and that society regards that as a crime? Conversely, if a defendant thought he was zapping space aliens, clearly, he would be legally insane.

---

[60] *Id.,* pp. 8-10.

[61] *Id.,* p. 11. The jury acquitted M'Nagthen; It is unlikely that a jury today would do so in the U.S.

[62] *Id.,* pp. 12-15.

Two later definitions were promulgated in the U.S. They incorporated medical concepts that, at trial, could lead to acquittal. In 1887 the first U.S. case, in Alabama, applied the "irresistible impulse" test. The "product of a mental disease or defect" standard first surfaced in an 1870 New Hampshire case; it was refined in the District of Columbia, per the Durham rule, which was used from 1954 to 1972.[63]

Both rules were considerably narrowed after the Hinckley acquittal. Each side presented multiple witnesses on the question of whether Hinckley was insane due to his having felt an "irresistible impulse" that caused him to shoot the president. In essence, the defense answered this in the affirmative, relying greatly on his infatuation with Jodie Foster, and consequent desire to impress her. The prosecution noted that Hinckley had decided when the president was strolling to the hotel entrance, not to shoot then, because the shooting angle was not good enough. Hence, to accept the argument made by the defense, jurors would have to conclude that Hinckley, having controlled his conduct at 1:45 PM, somehow lost his ability to control his conduct in the 45 minutes between the president's entry and his subsequent exit at 2:30 PM.[64]

Within three years of the 1982 acquittal verdict,[xxv] at a time when insanity claims were made in two percent of criminal cases and failed 75 percent of the time, Congress and half the states took decisive action to narrow such defenses: Congress

---

[63] *Id.*, pp 15-23. In a 1908 Canadian case, a judge rejected the "irresistible impulse" test, writing: *"If you cannot resist an impulse in any other way, we will hang a rope in front of your eyes, and perhaps that will help." Id., p. 17.*

[64] The arguments are discussed in exhaustive detail, *Id.*, pp. 24-132.

and nine states narrowed the substantive insanity test; Congress and nine states shifted the burden of proving insanity to the defense; eight states created a "guilty but insane" verdict option; and Utah abolished the insanity defense.[65]

In 2016, a federal judge ordered[xxvi] that Hinckley, then age 61, be released, ruling that he was no longer a threat.[66] Prior to the Hinckley case, two presidential assassination defendants formally lodged insanity pleas. In his trial for murdering president Garfield, Charles Guiteau failed to persuade the jury, and was hanged.[67] A partly different fate awaited defendant John Schrank, on trial for shooting Theodore Roosevelt. Schrank pleaded guilty to the charge of attempted murder. But the judge appointed a panel to assess Schrank's mental condition. The panel found Schrank insane, and the judge hence ruled that no jury could reasonably find otherwise. Schrank spent the rest of his life, 31 years, in a mental

---

[65] *Id.*, p. 140. Narrowing refers to stricter limits on what constitutes "irresistible impulse." Shifting the burden of proof means that pleading insanity is now what the law calls an "affirmative" defense, meaning that the defendant bears the burden of proof as to self-defense; typically, the standard of proof is by a "fair preponderance of the credible evidence." The "guilty but insane" verdict means that after a defendant serves his criminal sentence, he is remanded to the custody of a mental institution to receive treatment for his illness.

[66] *Id.*, pp. 155-206. Hinckley's release came in stages with each change reducing the amount of supervision and reporting requirements, beginning in 1999. Since 2016, Hinckley has been free without any supervision or reporting requirements.

[67] Rosenberg, Charles E.; *The Trial of the Assassin Guiteau: Psychiatry and Law in the Gilded Age* (Univ. of Chicago Press, 1968).

institution. During that time, Schrank never received a single letter or visitor.[68]

Reagan wound up politically profiting from his near miss, due to his widely reported aplomb at the hospital. He quipped to Parr, while he was being treated: "I hope they (the doctors) are all Republicans."[69] He wrote a note to his doctors, nurses and visitors after the operation from the recovery room "All in all, I'd rather be in Philadelphia."[70] His first words to Nancy Reagan were: "Honey, I forgot to duck!"[71] The public was under the impression that Reagan was immediately able to fully resume his presidential schedule. Medical briefings by GWU medical staff were upbeat, with no mention made of how close Reagan came to dying. But according to his personal physician, it was not until June 3 that Reagan worked a full day, and not until October that he told his doctor: "Now, I really feel like I'm all the way."[72]

Less remembered, but a big story for a few days, was the disastrous press conference held at the White House on March 30. At the White House, Deputy Press Secretary Larry Speakes, replacing his permanently disabled boss, was asked who had command of the nuclear codes, given that Vice-President Bush was on an airplane, flying back from Texas.

---

[68] Helferich, Gerald, *Theodore Roosevelt and the Assassin: Madness, Vengeance, and the Campaign of 1912*, pp. 223-31 (Lyons Press, 2013), pp. 240-42

[69] *Rawhide Down*, note 55 *supra*, p. 120.

[70] Feerick, John D., *The Twenty-Fifth Amendment: Its Complete History and Applications*, 3rd ed. (Ford. Univ. Press, 2014), p. 192.

[71] *Rawhide Down*, note 55 *supra*, p. 187.

[72] *The Twenty-Fifth Amendment*, 3rd ed., note 70 *supra*, p. 196.

The inexperienced Speakes was sputtering, looking like a deer caught in the headlights; he had no idea how to answer such a question. Downstairs in the White House Situation Room, meeting with other national security officials, the secretary of state, Alexander Haig, rushed upstairs into the press room, announcing that he was 'in control here" until Bush returned, and that if anything happened, he would check with the vice-president.

Unfortunately, Haig also said: "Constitutionally, you have the president, the vice-president and then the secretary of state, in that order." Haig, expert on national security matters—albeit later on, Defense Secretary Caspar Weinberger told Haig that he had also misstated the nation's alert status—was hardly one of the world's constitutional scholars. He had omitted the Speaker and president *pro tem*, both of whom, by statute, stood in front of Cabinet officials in the line of presidential succession. People more knowledgeable on the relevant laws sat downstairs, aghast, including attorney-general William French Smith. Haig, in his haste, was flustered as he took the podium, which amplified the negative impact of his well-intentioned effort.[73]

The only senior official who had done any contingency planning was White House counsel Fred Fielding, whose preliminary draft became the basis for handling future instances. Feerick notes that it remains unclear to what degree Vice-President Bush was involved; Bush, for his part, was scrupulous in avoiding even the appearance of being a usurper. He flew from Andrews AF Base to the vice-president's residence and then took a chopper to the White

[73] *Rawhide Down*, note 55 *supra*, pp. 171-77.

House South Lawn. He worked as Acting President from the vice-presidential office. The Haig kerfuffle proved a proverbial tempest in a teapot, thanks to the president's bravura performance.[74]

President George H. W. Bush

In April 1993 former president Bush visited Kuwait to speak at an event at Kuwait University celebrating the coalition victory in the Gulf War. A plot to assassinate him was hatched at the behest of Saddam Hussein, payback for assembling and leading the wartime coalition. Officials discovered a Toyota parked near the university, loaded with enough *plastique to* destroy anything within a quarter-mile radius. CIA bomb technicians concluded it was to be detonated by remote control as the Bush motorcade passed by.[75]

President George W. Bush

On May 10, 2005, Bush gave a speech in Tbilisi, Georgia. As Bush spoke, an assassin tossed a grenade towards the stand, where First Lady Laura Bush and the president and first lady of Georgia were seated behind the president. Though the grenade was live, the pin having been pulled, because the assassin had concealed it under a red tartan handkerchief wrapped around the grenade, the firing pin did not detonate fast enough to make the grenade explode; the grenade also was

---

[74] *Twenty-Fifth Amendment*, 3rd. ed., note 70 *supra*, pp. 193-97.

[75] *Killing the President*, note 38 *supra*, pp. 170-71. President Clinton ordered the launch of 23 Navy Tomahawk cruise missiles, targeting the Iraqi Intelligence Service. *Id.*

partially deflected because it struck a spectator, lessening its impact when it hit the ground.[76]

The Assassin's Violent Veto:

It is an oft uttered cliche that violence never solves anything. Tragically, that assertion is contradicted by actual events. One bad actor can alter the course of American—and world— history. The 1865 assassination of Lincoln delayed the true end of the Civil War by a full century, until passage of the 1964 civil rights and 1965 voting rights acts. Garfield's assassin failed in his attempt to kill civil service reform along with the president, as Garfield's successor, Chester Arthur, reversed course and supported his program.

McKinley's assassin, a deranged loner with deep but inchoate resentments, had no programmatic aim. Theodore Roosevelt's failed assassin wanted to prevent any president from serving a third term.[77] Had TR been wounded seriously enough—let alone, killed—voters in his Bull Moose Party likely would have voted for President Taft, who thus might have defeated Woodrow Wilson. In such event, Wilson's enormously consequential two terms, as America's first domestic Progressive and first international globalist president, would never have come to pass.

FDR's would-be assassin was desperately poor, and suffering from a chronically painful, then-incurable condition. Had his

---

[76] *Id.*, pp. 176-77.

[77] *Theodore Roosevelt and the Assassin*, note 68 *supra*, p. 224.

aim been steadier, the enormously consequential FDR presidency, which centralized power in Washington and spawned the executive branch's hypertrophic administrative bureaucracies, might never have in full extent come to pass. But the temper of the times—the Great Depression—made election of like-minded presidents likely, albeit no one else had FDR's charisma.

JFK's assassin, a disgruntled Marxist who had defected to the Soviet Union, only to be allowed (foolishly) to return to his native land, shattered America's confidence in a stable world order. It unleashed titanic forces domestically that began unravelling an America that had held an unparalleled world leadership status since the end of World War II.

June 8, 2022, saw a dangerous milestone in U.S. political assassinations: the attempted assassination of a U.S. Supreme Court justice. The would-be assassin, who turned himself in after being thwarted by marshals stationed at Brett Kavanaugh's residence, proclaimed[xxvii] in a Twitter exchange[xxviii] that he intended to kill up to three justices who were going to overturn *Roe v. Wade*. Doing so, he said, would change the Court "for decades to come." After presidents, only justices can have comparable long-term impact on the republic's fortunes. Hence, were a justice to be killed, it could be as big a news event, with enormous public impact, nearly comparable to that for a president. And other justices appointed by the same or similar presidents would become highest-value targets, likely with Secret Service protection.

The first-ever attempted assassination of a Supreme Court justice came as the administration declined to condemn unlawful protests outside several justices' homes.[78] In 2020, Senate Majority Leader Chuck Schumer had warned[xxix] two conservative justices, Kavanaugh and Neil Gorsuch, both appointed by President Trump, about overturning *Roe v. Wade*, on the very day the Court heard oral argument in *Dobbs v. Mississippi*, the case that ultimately led to the June 2022 decision overturning *Roe*:

> *I want to tell you, Justice Kavanaugh and Justice Gorsuch, you have unleashed a whirlwind, and you will pay the price. You won't know what hit you if you go forward with these awful decisions.*

By contrast, the assassination of others in the line of presidential succession—the Speaker of the House, Senate president *pro tem*, or Cabinet members—though a major media story, would not have nearly comparable impact on the republic's course. While tragic, there would be no partisan change of governing power in such cases.

Above all, what assassins accomplish in democracies is to veto the choice made by the electorate. This is enormously destabilizing, as democratic republics depend critically upon orderly transfers of power. Dictatorships do not; coups are normal incidents of political life. The attitudes of powerless masses are essentially irrelevant to their oppressive rulers.

Alternative history is, as the above examples show, a treacherous, highly speculative exercise. Tectonic events have

---

[78] Title 18, sec. 1507 of the U.S. criminal code, titled "Picketing and Parading," prohibits intimidation of judges, juries, witnesses, or court officers — near their place of work or their homes — in an effort to influence ongoing cases. Mob protests were staged at the homes of conservative justices in the immediate run-up to the June 24, 2022, release of the *Dobbs* decision.

secondary and tertiary consequences whose overall net result is rarely predictable. *But what is not at all conjecture is that countries where elections are the normal mode of choosing leaders can be dangerously destabilized by one bad actor in a single, horrific moment.*

PART II
PRESIDENTIAL DISABILITY
(1789-1960)

George Washington - Dwight Eisenhower

This second section covers highlights (and lowlights) of the history of presidential and vice-presidential disability in our constitutional republic, from 1789 to 1960, *i.e.*, the administrations from George Washington through Dwight David Eisenhower.

U.S. Constitution: Time Runs Out on Succession

Our story begins when the 1787 Grand Convention produced a Constitution that was a marvel, without equal on the planet, but also without fully addressing the grave issues attendant to presidential and vice-presidential disability. To be fair, the Framers were dealing with immense, complex and vexing issues of fundamental structure, distributing powers and rights, all from scratch, under time constraints. Given the grave shortcomings of the Articles of Confederation; a protracted debate on presidential and vice-presidential succession, with only our Colonial experience to guide the Framers, would likely have led nowhere. The question was neatly put by Framer John Dickinson of Delaware, on August 27, three weeks before the new Constitution was adopted: *"What is the extent of the term "disability" and who is to be the judge of it?"*[79]

The Framers addressed presidential and vice-presidential succession in Art. II, sec. 1, cl. 6, choosing language that proved

---

[79] *Failing Hands*, note 14 *supra*, p. 44. Feerick opines that although the word "Office" was chosen, that it was intended to refer to the vice-president as an Acting President, rather than holding the Office. This was ultimately clarified by sec. 3 of the 25th Amendment. *Id.*, p. 56.

to be ambiguous, with final resolution reached only with the 1967 ratification of the 25th Amendment:

> *In Case of the Removal of the President from Office, or of his Death, Resignation, or Inability to discharge the Powers and Duties of the said Office, the Same shall devolve on the Vice President, and the Congress may by law provide for the Case of Removal, Death, Resignation or Inability, both of the President and Vice President, declaring what Officer shall then act as President, and such Officer shall act accordingly, until the Disability be removed, or a President shall be elected.*

There was a modest amount of wrangling that summer over succession. The Constitution's[xxx] text includes Art. I, sec. 3, cl. 5:

> *The Senate shall choose their other Officers, and also a President pro tempore, in the absence of the Vice-President, or when he shall exercise the Office of President of the United States.*

In Federalist Paper 68, Alexander Hamilton makes passing reference to the role of the vice-presidency: "The appointment of an extraordinary person as vice-president, has been objected to as superfluous, if not mischievous … [T]he Vice-President may occasionally become a substitute for the President, in the extreme executive magistracy." Hamilton added that were a senator to fulfill that role, he would be trading a constant legislative vote for an occasional— "contingent"—tie-breaking vote.[80]

---

[80] The Federalist Papers, pp. 414-15 (Clinton Rossiter ed., Mentor Books, 1961).

A French expression, *saisir le bal au bond* —"seize the ball on the bounce"— best describes that hinge moment in history. Our "window of opportunity" metaphor is inadequate, in that it offers a static image that fails to capture the evanescence of the opportunity. The Latin *carpe diem* ("seize the day") has motion but lacks a visual image. Had the Framers missed in 1787, it might well have prevented the establishment of "a more perfect union"—at least, for decades; perhaps forever.

1804: Amendment XII Fills a Succession Gap.

The disputed election of 1800 required 36 ballots to settle on a president.[81] The prospect that a president might not be chosen by the March 4 inauguration led the Framers to insert a parenthetical provision in their revised method if choosing a president and vice-president:

> *(And if the House of Representatives shall not choose a president whenever the right of choice shall devolve upon them, before the fourth day of March next following, then* **the Vice-President shall act as president***, as in the case of the death, or other constitutional disability of the president.)*[82]

---

[81] *The Twenty-Fifth Amendment*, 25th Anny. ed., note 9 *supra*, p. 30. Feerick notes that there is some evidence suggesting that the Framers of the 12th Amendment believed that the vice-president would become president in the event of presidential inability. *Id.*, pp. 30-31.

[82] **U.S. Const.**, Amendment XII. This provision reinforces the counter-proposition that the Framers viewed the vice-president as merely an Acting President during periods of presidential inability. A more detailed discussion of these competing views is presented later in this Part.

Congress:
The 1792, 1886 and 1947 Succession Laws

1792: Congress Fills a Constitution Vacuum.

Ironically, while for a century the new republic had no provision for succession to the vice-presidency, during colonial times[83] there had been such arrangements.[84] Provinces had a governor and lieutenant governor; if both were vacant a governor's council (loosely equivalent to today's presidential Cabinet) or the senior councilor would step up. During the Colonial period, from Jamestown (1607) to ratification of the Articles of Confederation (1781), 40 out of 130—*i.e.*, one-third—of colonial governors had died in office. Feerick notes one especially interesting case, that of William Penn, founder of the state that bears his name. When he became senile, his second wife, Hannah, took the reins, continued to do so after her husband's death, until Penn's children attained adulthood.[85] This is exactly what Edith Bolling Galt, second wife of Woodrow Wilson, did for 17 months after her husband was laid low by a massive stroke; but heredity having been abolished as a means of automatic succession, her *de facto* regency ended March 4, 1921.

Nothing was done in the First Congress; Feerick notes that one member forecast that a double vacancy would not occur

---

[83] Descendants can of course be chosen by the voters, hence the presidencies of John Quincy Adams (1825-1829) and George W. Bush (2001-2009).

[84] *Failing Hands*, note 14 *supra*, pp. 23-38. For the 40/130 numbers, see *Id.*, p. 32.

[85] *Id.*, p. 29.

even once in a century; another member said that it would not happen more than once in *840 years*.[86] A double vacancy can be simultaneous—if in 1963 LBJ had been riding in the presidential limousine, instead of Governor John Connally.[87]

The Second Congress passed the first succession law in 1792. Section 10 of the 1792 law mandated a special election in event of a double vacancy; the state governors were to transmit slates of electors within 34 days of the third Wednesday in the following December.[88] (In 1792, and for long after, Congress was out of session most of every year.)

So, until 1886, the sole provision, per the 1792 statute, for presidential succession beyond the vice-presidency provided only for the Senate president *pro tem*, and then the Speaker of

---

[86] *The Twenty-Fifth Amendment*, 25th Anny. ed., note 9 *supra*, p. 37.

[87] Connally's gunshot wounds, if untreated quickly, could have been fatal. Connally, after feeling a bullet striking him in the back, cried: "Oh no, no, no. My God, they are going to kill us all." *From Failing Hands*, note 14 *supra*, pp. 4-5.

[88] *The Twenty-Fifth Amendment*, 25th Anny. ed., note 9 *supra*, p. 39. Feerick writes:

> *If less than two months remained before [the third Wednesday of the following December] and if the term of the President and Vice-President were not to end in the following March, the election would take place in December in the year next ensuing, with the newly elected President and Vice-President taking office in the following March. If the term were to end in March, no election at all would take place. The bill seems to have contemplated a four-year term for a specially-elected President and Vice-President.*

the House. *No Cabinet officers, nor any other persons, were in the line of presidential succession.*[89]

1886: Fixing 1792's Omission

The 1881 assassination of President James Garfield revived interest in changing the 1792 law. On Nov. 25, 1885, Grover Cleveland's vice-president, Thomas Hendricks, died[xxxi]. The office was vacant until Benjamin Harrison was inaugurated March 4, 1889. The 1792 law precluded Cleveland's choosing a new vice-president. The resourceful Cleveland did the next best thing: his first message to the incoming 49th Congress, in Dec. 1885, called for passage of a Senate bill passed earlier in 1885, that had died in the House. In 1886 he secured passage of a law rectifying the 1792 omission. The line of succession became the then-seven Cabinet officers, beginning with the Secretary of State, and then Treasury, War (renamed Defense in 1949), Attorney-General, Postmaster-General (abolished 1971), Secretary of the Navy (folded into Defense in 1949) and Secretary of the Interior. In event of a double vacancy, the top-ranked eligible secretary was to serve as Acting President until either: (a) the president's or vice-president's disability ended; or (b) a special election was called, and a new president and vice-president were elected; or (c) upon the end of the presidential term, on the next Inauguration Day.[90]

The debate was informed by the failed attempt to remove President Andrew Johnson in 1868. After the House voted

---

[89] *Failing Hands*, note 14 *supra*, pp. 57-62. The 1792 debate centered on whether placing members of Congress in the line of presidential succession would violate the separation of powers, by encroaching upon the prerogatives of the executive branch.

[90] *The Twenty-Fifth Amendment*, 25th Anny. ed., note 9 *supra*, pp. 40-42.

articles of impeachment, the Senate came within a single vote of convicting Johnson. Leading the Radical Republicans at the Senate trial was the Senate president *pro tem*, Senator Benjamin Wade of Ohio. With Johnson having succeeded the fallen Abraham Lincoln as president, the vice-presidency was vacant. Per the 1792 law the president *pro tem* stood in line ahead of the Speaker. It did not go unnoticed that Senator Wade was hardly a disinterested juror—nor, that one Democratic senator from Johnson's home state of Tennessee was the president's son-in-law.[91] The argument that party control might change was also aired in the deliberations, to no effect.[92] From 1886 through 1945, three presidents and two vice-presidents died in office, but fortunately, there was no double vacancy.[93]

Frequently, the opposition party has either controlled one or both Houses of Congress. In the 19th century this happened with 15 Congressional sessions, first in 1827; in the 20th, 20 times, first in 1913; and already in the 21st, 5 times, first in 2001.[94] The current Congress is the 118th[xxxii]. *Thus of 118 Congresses, 40 sessions—34 percent—have featured partisan division.* Presidents Ronald Reagan and George H.W. Bush, during their entire 12 consecutive years in office, never controlled both Houses.

---

[91] Rehnquist, William H., *Grand Inquests: The Historic Impeachments of Justice Samuel Chase and President Andrew Johnson*, p. 221 (William Morrow & Co, Inc., 1992).

[92] *The Twenty-Fifth Amendment*, 25th Anny. ed., note 9 *supra*, p. 214. Feerick notes that it was reported that Wade had already selected his Cabinet, before the final vote on removal was taken. *Id.*, p. 214, fn.

[93] *Id.*, pp. 42-45.

[94] *The Twenty-Fifth Amendment*, 3rd. ed., note 70 *supra*, Appendix E, pp. 315-16.

1947: Congress Returns to the Line of Succession

When Franklin Roosevelt died suddenly, less than 100 days into his fourth term, Harry Truman resolved to revise the 1886 law, by placing the Speaker and then the president *pro tem* back in the line of presidential succession. His stated reasons were: (a) all those in the line of succession should have been chosen democratically by the voters; (b) House members serve two-year terms, versus six years for senators, and hence they are more continually responsive to voter preferences; (c) though elected in a single Congressional district, the Speaker is the only officer, other than president and vice-president (albeit, from a different branch of government), who represents voters nationwide, via election as Speaker by a majority of votes in the House.[95]

Truman rejected the argument that voters in quadrennial presidential election years choose to be governed not simply by a president and vice-president, but also by an administration for the next four years. The off-year biennial elections amount to a mid-term grade on the administration's performance. Truman would not be swayed, even though the 1946 off-year elections put Republicans in charge of Congress, and he prevailed.[96]

As Senator Eugene McCarthy, put it in 1964:

> *The succession law should respect the mandate of the people, who vote not only for a man but also, in a broad way, for his party and his program. The elevation of a leader of another party in mid-term is*

---

[95] *The Twenty-Fifth Amendment*, 25th Anny. ed., note 9 *supra*, p. 42-46.

[96] *Id.*, p. 44-45.

undesirable in principle and could have most unfortunate practical effects.[97]

For his part, Senator Bayh, in retrospect, concurred:

One only has to imagine the divisiveness which would have been created had the White House been turned over to the opposing party in the person of the Speaker of the House to realize how significant an achievement this was.[98]

President Who???? To see the emerging danger, consider some of the Speakers and presidents *pro tem* that have served, since ratification of the 25th Amendment in 1967. Checking the list of House Speakers[xxxiii] reveals a group all regarded by the opposing party as intensely partisan and/or not a serious prospective president: Democrats John McCormack (MA), Carl Albert (OK), Tip O'Neill (MA), Jim Wright (TX), Tom Foley (WA), and Nancy Pelosi (CA); Republicans Newt Gingrich (GA) Denny Hastert (IL), John Boehner (OH), Paul Ryan (WI), Kevin McCarthy (CA) and Mike Johnson (LA).[99]

A list of Senate presidents *pro tem*[xxxiv] shows some (though fewer, given the tradition—now greatly eroded—of Senate collegiality) either regarded as partisan, under-qualified or far too elderly to carry the workload of the presidency. Most

---

[97] *Id.*, p. 73.

[98] *Id.*, Foreword.

[99] *Id.*, p. 237. Carl Albert, the Oklahoma Democrat who was Speaker from 1971-1977—during which time he faced two GOP presidents (Nixon and Ford)—reportedly said, when for a few months he was first in line of presidential succession (after the 1973 Agnew and 1974 Nixon resignations: "Lord help me, I pray every night it doesn't happen." *Id.*, p. 46.

notably were the cases of senators Strom Thurmond, *pro tem* at age 100, and Robert Byrd, *pro tem* at age 92. Unlike the office of Speaker (Art. I, sec. 2), the prime duty of presidents *pro tem* is to issue rulings on parliamentary procedure. Their presiding duties are largely ceremonial. The most important presiding task—breaking Senate tie votes—is given only to the vice-president, as president of the Senate (<u>U.S. Const.</u>, Art. I, sec. 3)[xxxv].

The wisdom of senators McCarthy and Bayh was borne out by the failure of reform efforts during Eisenhower's second term. Ike took the position in 1957 that the Cabinet, rather than anyone from Congress, should be next in line after the vice-president. But legislative leaders rejected the idea and did so again when the matter was raised anew after Eisenhower's late 1957 stroke. Put simply, they did not want to risk that Richard Nixon would become Acting President, were Eisenhower sidelined again, and a decision made to turn the reins over to Nixon, pending Ike's recovery.[100]

Other reform proposals included the idea of a special commission. Former president Truman published his idea in a New York Times article: a special commission consisting of the vice-president, chief justice, Speaker of the House, plus the majority and minority leaders of the House and Senate. The commission could appoint a medical panel to assess whether the president was well enough to continue in office; if the commissioners decided in the negative, the House and

---

[100] *Id.*, p. 22. In the event Eisenhower died or resigned, Nixon would have automatically ascended to the Oval office. Moreover, per the 22nd Amendment, with more than two years left in the president's term, Nixon, if he won in 1960, could have run again in 1964.

Senate could by a two-thirds vote remove the president.[101] Eisenhower's version would have established a medical commission, plus the Cabinet and the chief justice.[102] The idea of including any member of the judicial branch in presidential succession was scotched by Chief Justice Earl Warren, in a 1958 letter to Senate Judiciary Committee chairman Estes Kefauver. Writing on behalf of all the justices, Warren stated:

> *It has been the belief of all of us that because of the separation of powers in our Government. the nature of the judicial process, the possibility of a controversy of this character coming to the Court, and the danger of disqualification which might result in lack of a quorum, it would be inadvisable for any member of the Court to serve on such a commission.[103]*

Enacted as part of the landmark 1947 presidential succession statute[xxxvi], the law provides:

1. The vice-president assumes the "powers and duties" of the Presidency, as Acting President, in event of presidential inability; the Vice-President holds the Office

---

[101] *Id.*, p. 54.

[102] *Id.*, p. 22.

[103] *Id.*, p. 54, fn. Because the change might have been effected by a statute supplanting the 1947 succession law, rather than by the lengthy process of amending the Constitution, the Court would have had "arising under" jurisdiction, per U.S. Const. Art. III, sec. 2 ("The judicial power shall extend to all cases, in Law and Equity, arising under this Constitution, the laws of the United States...") As to disqualification, Warren's likely reference is to the need for justices to recuse themselves in event a president who appointed them became the subject of a disability inquiry. In Warren's case, that meant himself and Justice William Brennan. Per Title 28, U.S. Code sec. 1, a quorum for the High Court is six justices.

of the Presidency only if the president permanently relinquishes the Office of the Presidency (either voluntarily—by resignation or permanently disabling inability—or involuntarily: by House impeachment and Senate conviction, or by death).

2. Among others in the line of presidential succession, given a <u>double</u> vacancy, only the House Speaker and Senate president *pro tem* can serve as Acting President for the full remainder of a presidential term.

3. They can assume the powers and duties of the Presidency but cannot hold the Office of the Presidency.

4. If the elected president is *temporarily unable* to discharge the powers and duties of the Presidency, and there is no sitting vice-president, the Speaker or president *pro tem* serve as Acting President until the disabled president is able to resume serving as President.

5. Members of the Cabinet—in Constitutional parlance, "heads of the executive departments"—can <u>only serve</u> as Acting President. They stand in line of succession in the order that the departments were created. They can be "bumped" by a subsequent Speaker or president *pro tem*, who can then serve as Acting President for the remainder of the presidential term.

6. Speakers and presidents *pro tem* must irrevocably resign from Congress to become Acting President. A new Speaker cannot "bump" a president *pro tem* as Acting President.

7. There still is no line of statutory succession to the Vice-Presidency. In event of a VP vacancy, a sitting president holding the Office of the Presidency can nominate a prospective vice-president, who takes office upon confirmation by a majority in each House of Congress. If, after nominating a prospective vice-president, the President permanently leaves the Office of the

Presidency, and the President's nominee subsequently is confirmed as Vice-President, the new VP automatically bumps anyone below the VP in the line of presidential succession.

8. Under Art. II, section 1, cl. 5 of the U.S. Constitution[xxxvii], no one can qualify as Acting President unless they meet the requirements for presidents specified therein: *i.e.*, (a) they are a natural-born citizen; (b) at least 35 years old; and (c) have been 14 years a U.S. resident.[104]

Regarding points 1 and 2, these left a succession gap for 20 years, fixed by ratification of the 25th Amendment. Thus, when JFK was assassinated, his vice-president, LBJ, assumed the Presidency; but there was no settled procedure for filling a vice-presidential vacancy. This was fixed by sections 1 and 2 of the 25th Amendment (more on this in Part IV).[105]

Having set forth the Constitution and statutes extant and how they evolved from 1789 to 1960, we return to historical examples of president and vice-presidential succession, and problems encountered during those years.

From Washington through Taft (1789-1912). Through 1840, two vice-presidents died (George Clinton and Elbridge

---

[104] President Herbert Hoover returned from overseas in 1917, less than 14 years before winning the presidency in 1928. The Heritage Guide to the Constitution, p. 248, Regnery Publishing, 2nd edition., 2014.

[105] The full text of the 1947 law is at Title 3, U.S. Code, sec. 19. Titled "Vacancy in offices of both president and vice president; officers eligible to act," it specifies that such officers—House Speaker, Senate president *pro tem*, and "officers of the United States"—*i.e.*, members of the president's cabinet—become Acting President. As new departments are created, the presidential vacancy law is amended.

Gerry, both of whom served under James Madison). The only presidential disability of consequence occurred when for four months in 1813, Madison was sidelined with an illness never definitively diagnosed. In all, during Madison's two terms the nation was without a vice-president for over three years.[106] Clinton had become vice-president for Thomas Jefferson's second term (1805-1809), and then James Madison's first term (1809-1813), per the Twelfth Amendment[xxxviii]. Jefferson edged him in the electoral vote balloting for the presidency, so Clinton settled for being number two; Madison creamed Clinton in the balloting of 1808. A mortal adversary of both, and held in low regard, he died in 1811. His replacement, Elbridge Gerry, a strong Madison supporter, died in 1814.[107]

John C. Calhoun served as vice-president under John Quincy Adams (1825-1829) and during Andrew Jackson's first term (1829-1833), resigning late in 1832 to become a senator from South Carolina.[108]

The 1840s and 1850s were to provide several dramas. Exactly one month after his March 4, 1841, inaugural address, which ran more than two hours and was delivered in a cold rain. William Henry Harrison, who had not bothered to wear an overcoat, died of pneumonia. He was succeeded by John Tyler. Though not required by the Constitution to take an oath when ascending to the presidency—the Framers thought a vice-president having taken the vice-presidential oath sufficed—Tyler insisted on being formally sworn in,

---

[106] *Failing Hands,* note 14 *supra*, pp. 79-83.

[107] *Id.*

[108] *Id.*, pp. 85-86.

establishing a precedent followed since. A spirited debate ensued in both Houses of Congress as to whether Tyler should be called President, Vice-President, New President, or Acting President.[109]

A new succession crisis nearly arose on February 28, 1844. President Tyler took a group of cabinet officers, senators and foreign dignitaries on a Potomac River cruise on board the Navy's first propeller-driven warship, the *U.S.S. Princeton.* Guests were assembled *en masse* to witness a demonstration firing of the "Peacemaker," then the world's largest naval gun. The gun exploded, killing seven, including the secretaries of state and the Navy; 11 were wounded, including the ship's captain and one senator. Tyler, fortuitously, was below deck and emerged unscathed.[110]

In similar fashion as Tyler, Millard Fillmore succeeded Zachary Taylor on July 9, 1850, five days after "Old Rough and Ready" had sat for hours at a ceremony near the Washington Monument, under the broiling July sun; then upon returning to the White House, he had gorged himself on iced drinks and fruit. This gustatory combination caused acute indigestion, which developed into a fever. Vice-President Millard Fillmore was sworn in on July 10. The Senate selected a president *pro tem* on July 11, Democrat William King. The 1792 succession law placed the Senate president *pro tem* immediately behind the vice-president in the line of succession. But for one day—July 10—there was no president *pro tem.* Had Fillmore died on July 10, the only possible

---

[109] *Id.,* pp. 89-96. This was resolved with ratification of the 25th Amendment in 1967.

[110] *Id.,* p. 97.

successor would have been the Speaker of the House, Democrat Howell Cobb of Georgia. But Cobb was only 34, and thus Constitutionally ineligible (under age 35) to ascend to the presidency. As Cabinet officers were not added to the succession line until 1886, *for one day there would have been no head of the executive branch.*[111]

When Democrat Franklin Pierce was elected in 1852, his vice-president, the aforementioned King, was elderly and infirm. He died on March 24, 1853, 20 days into his term. At the time, Pierce was ill with malaria, an illness which persisted for several months; *had Pierce died, there would have been a double vacancy.* The vice-presidential office was vacant until March 4, 1857, when Democrat James Buchanan became president, and John Breckenridge—at 36 the youngest ever to hold the office—became vice-president.[112] In 1865, Andrew Johnson followed the Tyler presidential oath script for vice-presidents ascending to the presidency, upon Lincoln's murder. This permanently established the practice.[113]

The first protracted succession crisis came with the shooting of James Garfield on July 2, 1881. Vice-President Chester Arthur, who had never held office higher than New York City port commissioner, became president. When he first heard the news Arthur exclaimed "I hope—my God, I do hope it is a

---

[111] *Id.*, pp. 99-104.

[112] *Id.*, pp. 104-07.

[113] *Id.*, p. 111.

mistake!"[114] Arthur's tenure was marked by serious health problems. In April 1883 he suffered a severe abdominal attack whose effects were minimized when press inquiries ensued.[115] Arthur's 1883 decision not to seek a full term as president was driven by his having been diagnosed with Bright's Disease, a chronic nephritis—inflammation of his kidney blood vessels—which took his life in 1886.[116]

At the time not only did the vice-presidency become vacant upon Arthur's accession, but the offices of president *pro tem* of the Senate and Speaker of the House, the only others in line of presidential succession per the 1792 presidential succession law, were both vacant. Had Arthur died before Grover Cleveland and Vice-President Thomas Hendricks were sworn in on March 4, 1885, per the 1792 law the only procedure available was to call a special election.

Cleveland's second term (non-consecutive) was marked in early 1893 by his developing a cancerous tumor in his right jaw while on vacation. He underwent emergency surgery, during which part of his jaw was removed, to be replaced by an artificial implant. It was five weeks before he returned to Washington. Of this drama not only was the public unaware;

---

[114] Greenberger, Scott S., *The Unexpected President: The Life and Times of Chester A. Arthur*, (Da Capo Press, 2017), p. 172. Arthur was sworn in after midnight by a New York judge. *Id.*, p. 173. Later that day, in Washington, D.C., he was sworn in by Chief Justice Morrison Waite. *Id.*, p. 175.

[115] *Id.*, pp. 214-16.

[116] *Id.*, p. 227. For more on the ailment, see the Mayo Clinic's nephritis webpage.

only one member of the Cabinet knew.[117] Worse, Vice-President Adlai Stevenson (whose son was to lose twice to Eisenhower, six decades later) was kept in the dark. It was not until 1917 that the episode was made public.[118] By then the McKinley and TR events had transpired.

Woodrow Wilson 1919-1921: President in Name Only.

Woodrow Wilson fell ill on Sept. 25, 1919. He returned to Washington on Sept. 28, and on Oct. 2 he was laid low by a massive stroke that paralyzed his left side. Thus ended any serious chance of Wilson's achieving his cherished twin foreign policy goals, ratification of the Treaty of Versailles and U.S. entry into the League of Nations—albeit, both battles were already steeply uphill.[119]

For more than six months Wilson hardly saw anyone, and was only able to do very limited work for the remainder of his term. A triumvirate took over: First Lady Edith Bolling Galt, the prominent socialite and second wife of Wilson; his private secretary Joseph Tumulty; and his physician, Dr. Cary

---

[117] Jeffers, H. Paul, *An Honest President: The Life and Presidencies of Grover Cleveland*, pp. 269-73 (William Morrow, 2000). A 1902 accidental fall from his horse-drawn carriage left Pres. Roosevelt with injuries requiring emergency surgery. *Planning for Emergency Threats: Rethinking the Presidential Line of Succession,* Ascher, Gregory, Nakhla, Myrna & Shea, Colin*,* Fordham Law School Rule of Law Clinic, p. 4 (August 2022).

[118] *The Twenty-Fifth Amendment*, 25th Anny. ed., note 9 *supra*, pp. 11-12.

[119] Heckscher, August, *Woodrow Wilson* (Collier Books, Macmillan Publishing Co., 1991), p. 589. Wilson was adamant that Article X of the Versailles Treaty, under which members of the League of Nations were obligated to come to the aid of any member whose political independence was endangered, and to defend them against acts of aggression, be accepted without modification by the senators. His Republican opponents would not accept these.

Grayson. Thus, began what amounted to a *sub-silento* regency. A few Cabinet members knew—notably, Secretary of State Robert Lansing, who confronted Tumulty and Grayson the day after the president's massive stroke. He told them that the vice-president should step in, per the Constitution's 12th Amendment— "in the case of the death or other constitutional disability of the president"—given Wilson's manifest inability to carry on. Asked by Tumulty who would decide Wilson's inability, Lansing replied that he, Tumulty and Grayson should do so. Tumulty and Grayson adamantly refused, saying that to do so would be an act of disloyalty to someone who had treated them well. By October 4, Grayson had concluded that Wilson would never recover.[120]

Lansing, who along with the Cabinet helped the triumvirate carry on some routine matters, urged Wilson to step aside, but he refused. Matters came to a head in February 1920, with an exchange of letters between Wilson—or someone writing on his behalf—and Lansing. Accused of disloyalty for running Cabinet meetings without presidential approval, Lansing offered his resignation, which Wilson accepted. It is unclear whether Lansing's resignation was truly voluntary or demanded by the president. *Making matters worse is that, as many outside observers noted, there is zero Constitutional authority reserved solely to the president as to calling Cabinet meetings. No express Constitutional authority exists in the document, as to this subject.*[121]

Historian August Heckscher, in his magisterial biography, wrote that Wilson's collapse had been preceded by warning signs for decades. As early as 1896 he had endured episodes

---

[120] *Failing Hands*, note 14 *supra* pp. 162-67

[121] *Id.*, pp. 176-79.

of "neuralgia," and in 1906 he suffered a stroke that left him blind in one eye. In the run-up the final sequence of strokes that felled him he was hit with a series of transient ischemic attacks (TIA, *i.e.*, mini-strokes).[122] Heckscher wrote: "Thus begun, with the silent assent of some, with the active maneuvering of others, such a coverup as American history had not known before."[123]

Vice-President Thomas Marshall, whom Wilson thought "a small-calibre man," was kept in the dark. For his part, Marshall was in no mood to accept designation as Acting President, fearful of the First Lady. Reputedly said he: "I am not going to get myself entangled with . . . the wife of the president of the United States."[124]

Lansing, for his part, convened the Cabinet some twenty times during the worst months of Wilson's illness, to make essential decisions—many of them routine but necessary to keep the government running. Feerick dispels the idea that there was nothing of great importance that went undecided during Wilson's remaining months in office: no presidential appointments of executive branch officials or federal judges could be made; 28 legislative bills passed because Wilson could

---

[122] *Woodrow Wilson*, note 119 *supra*, pp. 612.

[123] *Id.*, p. 613.

[124] *Failing Hands*, note 14 *supra*, p. 176. Wilson's "small calibre man" description is at *Woodrow Wilson*, fn. 119, *supra*, p. 615.

not exercise the option—his alone—to veto them in the 10-day period after they reached his desk.[125]

Not until March 4, 1921, after 17 months, did America have a president, Warren G. Harding, chosen by the electorate.

Because there is archival film footage of Wilson's presidency, there is a temptation to regard his tenure as a modern presidency. Yet this was hardly the case. The first transcontinental telephone call was made in January 1915.[126] It was not until November 2, 1920—exactly 13 months after Wilson suffered his disabling stroke—that the first commercial broadcast radio station went on the air, in Detroit.[127] True nationwide broadcast radio made FDR the first radio president. And it was not until the presidency of Harry Truman that, in 1948, the first regular over-the-air nationwide broadcast television programs made their debut.[128]

When Calvin Coolidge was offered the vice-presidential slot on the 1920 Republican ticket, his principal supporter urged him to decline the nomination, because Coolidge "might be shelved politically" and also because "idle life" might kill him. Warren Harding was stricken in late July 1923 while on tour,

---

[125] *Failing Hands,* note 14 supra, p. 175. Vice-President Marshall could not do so, because he had *no express Constitutional right to act as president* when Wilson was disabled. This was ultimately fixed by Section 3 of the 25th Amendment.

[126] *Events in Telecommunications History*, pp. 20-23 (AT&T Historical Archives ed., 1983).

[127] *Id.*

[128] Sterling, Christopher H. and Kittross, John Michael, *Stay Tuned: A History of American Broadcasting*, pp. 302-12 (Lawrence Erlbaum Associates, 3rd ed., 2002). The first true television president was John F. Kennedy. *Id.*, pp. 475-77.

succumbing to cerebral thrombosis (blood clot) on August 2. At which point "idle life" ended for now-president Coolidge, until March 4, 1929, when Herbert Hoover was inaugurated.[129]

Fast forward to January 1945. FDR's Inaugural Address, delivered from the south portico of the White House, seated, lasted less than five minutes. On January 22 he departed for the summit to be held at Yalta, a Russian resort by the Black Sea. The conference entailed crossing the Atlantic Ocean and Mediterranean Sea by boat, and flying between Cairo and Yalta. In all, the trip took three weeks, ending February 11. At Yalta, FDR made major concessions to Soviet dictator Joseph Stalin, partly reflecting the Red Army's superior military position in Eastern Europe, and partly because his personal priority was the creation of the United Nations, which he saw as the first step towards eventual world government. The UN conference was set for April 25, and FDR planned to attend. Taking much-needed rest at his home in Warm Springs, Georgia, on April 12 he died of a massive cerebral hemorrhage.[130] FDR's physicians had examined him in early 1944 and realized he was gravely ill, but the diagnosis was not even shared with FDR's family.[131] When Harry Truman was summoned to the White House and told by First Lady Eleanor Roosevelt that FDR had died, Truman asked if there was anything he could do for her. To which she replied, "Is there

---

[129] *Failing Hands*, note 14 *supra*, pp. 181-186.

[130] Miller, Nathan, *FDR: An Intimate History* (Madison Books, 1983), pp. 502-10.

[131] *Failing Hands, note 14 supra*, p.195.

anything we can do for you? Because you are the one in trouble now."[132]

Dwight Eisenhower's eight years were marked by three notable health crises in his second term. "Ike" had a heart attack on September 24, 1955, and could not meet with his Cabinet for two months. He did not return full-time until January 16, 1956. On June 9, Ike had surgery to remove an obstruction in his intestine; it was two months before he could resume a full schedule. On November 25, 1957, Ike had a stroke which temporarily affected his speech, but on December 2 he was back at work. During these serial crises Vice-President Nixon, the Cabinet and White House chief of Staff Sherman Adams ran things in an open, orderly fashion— in stark contrast to the simmering conflicts, major breakdowns and secrecy that paralyzed the Wilson administration and repeatedly misled the public for 17 months.[133]

Early into his last ordeal, Ike told his inner circle: "If I cannot attend to my duties, I am simply going to give up this job. Now, that is all there is to it." Sherman Adams then alerted

---

[132] *Id.*, note 14 *supra*, p. 197. That Truman faced huge challenges shows that Eleanor Roosevelt knew of which she spoke. No doubt the weight of all those troubles played a large role in Truman's declining to seek a third term. Though the 22nd Amendment was ratified in 1951, sec. 1 explicitly exempted from its operation a president who held the office when the Amendment was proposed in 1947, through its ratification. Thus, Eisenhower was the first president limited to two terms. A president who serves more than two years of a term after being elevated to the presidency—in other words, after a duly elected president dies, resigns, or is impeached and then removed from office—is considered that have served one term, and can only be re-elected for one more term.

[133] *The Twenty-Fifth Amendment*, 25th Anny. ed., note 9 *supra*, pp. 17-22.

Nixon that he might become president in 24 hours.[134] The popular Ike finished his second term, but unbeknownst to all at the time, the world stage was set for the political shock of a lifetime.

Eisenhower, for his part, took the proverbial bull by the horns, writing a letter to Vice-President Nixon, acting Attorney-General William P. Rogers, and Secretary of State John Foster Dulles, made public on March 3, 1958:

> *(1) In the event of inability, the President would—if possible—so inform the Vice-President, and the Vice President would serve as Acting President, exercising the powers and duties of the office until the inability had ended.*
>
> *(2) In event of an inability which would prevent the President from communicating with the Vice-President, the Vice-President, after such consultation as seems to him appropriate under the circumstances, would decide upon the devolution of the powers and duties of the Office and would serve as Acting President until the inability had ended.*
>
> *(3) The President, in either event, would determine when the inability had ended and at that time would resume the full exercise of the powers and duties of the Office.*[135]

This letter—in effect, a memorandum of understanding among the parties, was subsequently adopted by the Kennedy administration, between President Kennedy and Vice-President Lyndon Johnson, and then, between LBJ, his Vice-

---

[134] *Id.,* p. 21.

[135] *Id.,* pp. 55-56.

President Hubert Humphrey and House Speaker John McCormack.[136]

Conclusion: To date, we have managed succession fairly well, with the signal exception of the Lincoln assassination. That unleashed demons that dashed Lincoln's hopes for an aftermath to America's most ruinous war that, "with malice towards none and charity for all," would "bind up the nation's wounds." Today's emerging grave crisis comes at a time that evinces the most savage domestic partisanship since the Civil War, exacerbated by the malignant accelerants of mass and social media. Society is still reeling from Pandemic Hell, and Summer 2020's protracted orgiastic rioting. The latter triggered nationwide destruction of once-revered national symbols, and left whole sections of major American cities devastated, with spiraling crime and sputtering economies. Never in this author's long life—not even at the height of the Cold War, save for the transient harrowing second week of 1962's Cuban Missile Crisis[xxxix], after President Kennedy first informed the public in a televised address—has the famed first verse of William Butler Yeats's poem, The Second Coming (1919)[xl], seemed more apt:

Turning and turning in the widening gyre
The falcon cannot hear the falconer;
Things fall apart; the centre cannot hold;
Mere anarchy is loosed upon the world,
The blood-dimmed tide is loosed, and everywhere
The ceremony of innocence is drowned;
The best lack all conviction, while the worst
Are full of passionate intensity.

---

[136] *Id.*, p. 56. These formulations laid the foundation for what later became the 25th Amendment.

In an historical coincidence, 1919 also marked the first great 20th century leadership crisis in America, that being the year that Woodrow Wilson suffered his debilitating stroke. Then, in 1945, came Franklin Roosevelt's death, less than 100 days into a term for which he should never have run; it left Vice-President Harry Truman scandalously unprepared by the dying FDR, who had never even told Truman about the atom bomb.[137] Fortunately, Truman rose to the occasion. The third crisis was after JFK's assassination. Lyndon Johnson managed an awkward, painful transition well, and without the formal guidance that a Constitutional Amendment would have provided. (This transition evaluation, widely shared, is of a stand-alone task; the immense and tragic consequences of the assassination still reverberate. Part IV will include an assessment of the longer-term impact.)

So, in the nearly 175 years from April 30, 1789, through November 21, 1963, several times by narrow margins, America had weathered major presidential health crises, albeit not without key business at times being delayed or not getting done at all. Our luck was about to change.

Came Friday, November 22, 1963. America's lucky streak ended on a sunny day in Dallas. The impact upon the American polity was captured in an exchange between Washington Post columnist Mary McGrory and Daniel Patrick Moynihan, then an assistant secretary of labor. She

---

[137] *Truman*, note 50 *supra*, p. 348. Secretary of War Henry Stimson told Truman the evening of April 12, hours after FDR died, that the U.S. was working on a new explosive of unbelievable power. As it was not until July 16 that the "Trinity" test proved that the atomic bomb worked, that was all Stimson could say.

recalled[xli] saying to Moynihan: "We will never laugh again." Moynihan replied: "Mary, we'll laugh again, but we'll never be young again."

PART III
THE 25TH AMENDMENT (1961-67)

Part I covered what I've chosen to call "the assassin's veto": the ability of a single malefactor to nullify millions of votes by a single criminal act, an event profoundly destabilizing in democratic republics. Part II covered historical precedents from the republic's 1789 birth to the end of President Eisenhower's tenure. Part III offers an historical note, then covers the Kennedy-Johnson years, when events pushed the president and Congress towards adopting the 25th Amendment to stabilize presidential succession.

The Framers' Heritage (1787-1937)

Historically antecedent to the serial deaths and disabilities of presidents and vice-presidents was how the 1787 Grand Convention dealt with succession issues. The vice-presidency was minimally covered during the 3-1/2 months in Philadelphia. The vice-president, a member of the executive branch, would be the *ex officio* president of the Senate; in event of presidential disability or death, he would succeed the president. Although not explicit in the original Constitutional language, the Framers debated the distinction between a temporary acting president, and a permanent successor president. The debate could not be settled at the time.

This confusion prevailed for 150 years, until superseded by Section 3 of the 20th Amendment[xlii], ratified January 23, 1933, but not effective until January 1937, when the new Congress assembled January 3, and the new president was inaugurated January 20. Section 3 provides:

> *If, at the time fixed for the beginning of the term of the President, the President elect shall have died, the Vice President elect shall become*

75

president. If a President shall not have been chosen before the time fixed for the beginning of his term, or if the President elect shall have failed to qualify, then the Vice President elect **shall act as** *President until a President shall have qualified; and the Congress may by law provide for the case wherein neither the President elect nor a Vice President shall have qualified, declaring who* **shall then act as** *President, or the manner in which one who is to act shall be selected, and such person* **shall act accordingly** *until a President or Vice President shall have qualified.*

Turning Point: JFK's Thousand Days (1961-1963)

The ascension of John Fitzgerald Kennedy as 35th president of the United States, on Jan. 20, 1961, was an especially festive occasion. The first Inaugural telecast nationwide, its audience was swelled by viewers on the eastern seaboard, much of which was blanketed by a blizzard in the preceding 24 hours. A seemingly vigorous president, 27 years—a generation—younger than the elderly man he replaced, stepped up to the microphone to deliver[xliii] what has since been widely recognized as one of the greatest inaugural addresses.

On June 11, 1963, Senator Estes Kefauver, Adlai Stevenson's running mate in 1956, said of solving the problems of presidential succession after the Eisenhower health scares:

> *We are very fortunate that this country now has a young, vigorous and obviously healthy president. This will allow us to explore these problems in detail without any implication that the present holder of that high office is not in good health.*[138]

---

[138] *The Twenty-Fifth Amendment*, 25th Anny. ed., note 9 *supra*, p. 51.

Kennedy's apparent robust health was fiction: he suffered from numerous maladies, some known—his back troubles; others unknown—his having Addison's disease[xliv], a rare malady, potentially fatal, in which the adrenal glands develop hormonal—and, hence, functional—insufficiency. JFK was philosophical about the risk of assassination, saying[xlv] matter-of-factly: "If anyone is crazy enough to want to kill a president of the United States, he can do it. All he must be prepared to do is give his life for the president's."

In his book on the assassination author Gerald Posner recounts the chaotic aftermath of the shooting and JFK's having been pronounced dead at Parkland Hospital. The president's body was to be flown back to the Capitol on Air Force One with President Lyndon Johnson and First Lady Jacqueline Kennedy. But the Dallas authorities stated that they would first perform an autopsy in Dallas, before allowing shipment. LBJ would not leave without the casket, and Mrs. Kennedy wouldn't leave the hospital without her husband's body. A tense confrontation with the Secret Service ensued, with the agency prepared to force the issue. Unknown to those outside the hospital, the doctor in charge of the emergency room had authorized removal. In the event, violence was averted, and before takeoff LBJ was sworn in on Air Force One by friend and federal judge Sarah Hughes.[139]

The assassination revived concerns about serious gaps in the laws governing presidential disability, expressed succinctly by

---

[139] Posner, Gerald, *Case Closed: Lee Harvey Oswald and the Assassination of JFK*, pp. 294-95 (Random House, 1993).

New York Times columnist James Reston, writing on[xlvi] Nov. 23:

> *For an all too brief hour today, it is not clear again what would have happened if the young president, instead of being mortally wounded, had lingered for a long time between life and death, strong enough to survive but too weak to govern.*

For his part, Senator Kenneth Keating (R-NY), said at a Senate hearing convened after JFK's death:

> *As distasteful as it is to entertain the thought, a matter of inches spelled the difference between the painless death of John F. Kennedy and the possibility of his permanent incapacity to exercise the duties of the highest office of the land.*[140]

Less than one month after JFK's murder, Senator Bayh summed up the reasons to move with dispatch:

> *The accelerated pace of international affairs, plus the overwhelming problems of modern military security, make almost imperative that we change our system to provide for not only a President but a Vice President at all times.*
>
> *The modern concept of the Vice President is that of a man "standing in the wings"—even if reluctantly—ready at all times to take the burden. He must know the job of the President. He must keep current on all national and international developments. He must, in fact, be something of an "assistant President..."*[141]

---

[140] *The Twenty-Fifth Amendment*, 25th Anny. ed., note 9 *supra*, p. 57.

[141] *Id.*, pp. 65-66. Senator Bayh's statement was made on December 12, 1963.

LBJ fully understood all this and made shepherding a constitutional amendment covering presidential and (with limits discussed below) vice-presidential succession, a priority, from proposal through final ratification. In his November 27 special message to Congress five days after Dallas, with no sitting vice-president, a nationwide television audience saw LBJ speaking from the House chamber. The new president was flanked by House Speaker John McCormack (D-MA), age 71 and Senate president *pro tem* Carl Hayden (R-AZ), age 86.[142]

The 25th Amendment Emerges (1964-1967)

By February 1964 there had emerged a consensus that a Constitutional amendment was the way to go, and on its broad outlines: (1) in event of presidential disability, the vice-president should be Acting President, but not hold the Office of President; (2) if the President permanently departs—death, resignation or removal—the new President must nominate a new Vice-President, subject to confirmation by Congress; (3) declarations in connection with presidential disability and termination of same must be in writing; (4) involuntary presidential disability must be decided by the Vice-President, and the Cabinet, or of such other body as Congress may by law provide.[143]

The value of this language is that it resolved one of the main points of disputation in the period 1956 to 1964: Between those who wanted the succession laws embedded in a

---

[142] *One Heartbeat Away*, note 2 *supra*, pp. 8-9. JFK's term saw the death of two persons: one often in the presidential line of succession: Speaker Sam Rayburn (Nov. 1961) and 1956-VP nominee Sen. Estes Kefauver (Aug. 1963), who if elected would have been first in line. *Id.*, p. 113.

[143] *The Twenty-Fifth Amendment*, 25th Anny. ed., note 9 *supra*, pp. 60-61.

Constitutional amendment, so that passions of the moment did not enable a temporary partisan majority in Congress to expediently change the existing law, and those who feared that putting too many detailed requirements into an amendment would deprive decision makers of necessary flexibility, given that no one can anticipate the full variety of circumstances that might arise.

One idea floated in 1964 that was almost unanimously rejected was to restore the 1792 succession law's provision for a special election in case all those in the statutory line of succession—then only two—were unable to step in. The consensus was that a national special election today would be far too time-consuming to implement, in an era of rapidly unfolding events.[144]

An idea many witnesses endorsed was altering the 1947 presidential succession statute to take the Speaker and president *pro tem* out of the line of succession; celebrated historian Clinton Rossiter called that law "a poor one, in many ways one of the poorest ever to emerge from this stately and distinguished body."[145]

As noted above, the 1947 presidential succession law created the potential for serious conflict at a time when stability is most needed. Placing the Speaker of the House and president

---

[144] *Id.*, pp. 71-72. One prominent objector was then-American Bar Association President Lewis Powell, who was to be elevated by to the Supreme Court by President Nixon in 1971, where he was to serve until his retirement in 1987. Powell called a new election idea "a new and drastic departure from our historic system of quadrennial presidential elections and would introduce various complications into our political structure." *Id.*, p. 72.

[145] *Id.*, p. 73.

pro tem of the Senate immediately after the vice-president and before any member of the president's Cabinet—in Constitutional parlance, "officers of the executive departments"[146] — risks having an administration being turned over to the opposition party, in stark contravention of voter preference expressed in the polling booth.[147]

Bayh explained that the Committee decided for two reasons to abandon any effort to change the 1947 law. First, Congress had failed to pass any measure since 1947, whether amending the Constitution or revising the statute, and hence asking Congress to pass both was unrealistic. Second, if it came down to an either/or choice, revising the 1947 law would pass, as nothing would be encased in a Constitutional amendment.[148]

Former vice-president Nixon told the Committee that during his eight years as Eisenhower's vice-president he had cast a tie-breaking vote in the Senate on average once per year. He added, as to the vice-president's primary roles:

---

[146] *Id.*, Appendix A, p. 245, sec. 4, final form.

[147] See comments of senators McCarthy, *Id.*, p. 73 and Bayh, *Id.*, Foreword. Truman wanted to appear before the Senate to testify on behalf of his 1947 law or, alternatively, place a letter in the record. But the Committee, having firmly decided to avoid the 1947 succession law debate, decided not to accept either, of which Bayh noted: "It could not help us, and we did not want to embarrass the former president." *One Heartbeat Away*, note 2 *supra*, pp. 60-61.

[148] Early on, it became clear that repealing the 1947 law was a non-starter. *Change Doubted in Succession Law: Senate Panel Narrows Hunt for Solution on Presidency* (New York Times, p. 40, March 15, 1964). Bayh knew when to fold his cards. Goldstein, Joel K, Birch Bayh and the Twenty-Fifth Amendment: Lessons in Leadership. vol. 89, Fordham Law Review, p. 51 (2020).

First, his participation in the deliberations of the National Security Council; his participation in the deliberations of the Cabinet; and then the increasingly great use of the Vice-President as a trouble-shooter and as a representative of the President abroad in the field of foreign policy.[149]

On August 5, 1964, 65 senators voted unanimously to report out Senate Judiciary Resolution 139. It was the first-ever proposal to address presidential inability and vice-presidential vacancy. It was passed despite knowing that the House would not consider the measure. But its passage provided much of the spadework that would be used in 1965 as an integral part of the Congress would do in order to pass an amendment that could be sent to the States for ultimate ratification.[150]

On January 20, 1965, when Hubert Humphrey became vice-president, this problem was resolved. Both the House and Senate, albeit with slightly differing versions, had introduced new bills in the first week of the new administration, signaling their importance by designating them H.R. 1 and S. 1. Johnson, who had declared his intention to update presidential succession laws in his January 4 State of the Union address, endorsed their proposals on January 28, calling for prompt passage:

Favorable action by the Congress on the measures here recommended will, I believe, assure the orderly continuity in the Presidency that is imperative to the success and stability of our system. Action on these measures now will allay future anxiety among our own people, and

---

[149] *One Heartbeat Away*, note 2 *supra*, p. 87.

[150] Feerick, John D., The Proposed Twenty-Fifth Amendment to the Constitution, 34 Fordham Law. Rev. 173, vol. 34, Issue 2, p. 186 (1965)

among the peoples of the world, in the event senseless tragedy or unforeseeable disability should strike again at either or both of the principal Offices of our constitutional system. If we act now, without undue delay, we shall have moved closer to achieving perfection of the great constitutional document on which the strength and success of our system have rested for nearly two centuries.[151]

Concerns were raised anew in the Senate debates as to whether when Congress is controlled by the opposition party it might refuse to confirm a new vice-president, so that the Speaker would be next in line if the new president fell by the wayside. To which Bayh responded:

I have more faith in the Congress acting in an emergency in the white heat of publicity, with the American people looking on. The last thing Congress would dare to do would be to become involved in a purely political move.[152]

For his part, Senator Sam Ervin (D-SC), revered as a scholar of the Constitution, said:

---

[151] *The Twenty-Fifth Amendment*, 25th Anny. ed., note 9 *supra*, pp. 83-84. On September 29, 1964, the Senate had unanimously passed (65-0) its version of the 25th Amendment. But the House had declined to act, because with no sitting vice-president, its members felt that passage under such circumstances would imply that the Speaker—next in line of succession given that there was no vice-president—was somehow unsuited to become president. Realizing that, the Senate had stripped its proposal of anything regarding the 1947 statute as to succession by the Speaker or Senate president *pro tem. Id.*, pp. 73-74.

[152] *Id.*, p. 93.

God help this nation if we ever get a House of Representatives, or a Senate, which will wait for a President to die so someone whom they love more than their country will succeed to the Presidency.[153]

A final point of concern was the initial requirement in Section 4 that Congress must assemble within 48 hours in event of a case of involuntary presidential disability, as a large-scale attack could render rapid assembly impossible.[154] In 1965 assembly meant physical presence; but since the Covid pandemic, former House Speaker Nancy Pelosi, with rare exceptions, allowed proxy voting by those physically present, on behalf of others not attending; in 2023 Speaker Mike Johnson abolished Pelosi's Covid rule. Proxy voting, if the House were to amend its rules, could be reinstated, and expanded to permit full virtual assembly from remote locations during emergency conditions.

On June 30, 1965, the House passed the bill as reported out of the House-Senate conference, by a vote of 368 to 29. On

---

[153] *Id.*, p. 94. Two senators who were not sure of this, Robert Kennedy (D-NY) and Philip Hart (D-MI), suggested that the Cabinet and vice-president might stage a coup, per the false pretext that the president was disabled. When Rhode Island senator John Pastore (D) responded that the Cabinet would have been picked by the very president they would one asked to depose, RFK replied that (excepting himself) JFK had not known personally any of the members of his Cabinet. *One Heartbeat Away*, note 2 *supra*, p. 263.

[154] *Id.*, p. 283. RFK also raised the specter of a split Cabinet, arising out of a presidential disability dispute, with one faction backing the president and another backing the vice-president. to which Senator McCarthy suggested that it could resemble the lengthy medieval conflict between the Catholic Popes in Rome and the French Anti-Popes at Avignon. *Id.*, p. 310.

July 6, the Senate followed suit, by a vote of 68 to 5.[155] The 25th Amendment was then sent to the States for ratification.[156]

State ratification votes cascaded in a veritable avalanche of support, with little opposition. By the end of 1965 ten states had ratified; within one year 30 states had done so. On February 10, 1967, the 38th state ratified, making the 25th Amendment part of the Constitution.[157] On February 23, President Johnson said, at a White House ceremony celebrating ratification:

> *Once, perhaps, we could pay the price of inaction. But today in this crisis-ridden era there is no margin for delay, no possible justification for ever permitting a vacuum in our national leadership. Now, at last,*

---

[155] *The Twenty-Fifth Amendment*, 25th Anny. ed., note 9 *supra*, p. 107. Ironically, Walter Mondale, in his first year as a Minnesota senator—an appointed one, not to be elected in his own right until 1966—was one of the five senators who voted against passage, along with Minnesota's other senator, Democrat Eugene McCarthy, then in his second term. Bayh noted in his memoir that Mondale was "obviously reluctant to oppose his senior colleague." *One Heartbeat Away*, note 2 *supra*, p. 332. In 2021, Jonathan Alter wrote in the Washington Monthly that Mondale rose to become an enormously consequential vice-president: first to lunch weekly with the president, first with walk-in privileges to the Oval Office, and first to be put in the military chain of command. President Carter told his staff: "If you get an order from Fritz, it's as if it's an order from me." *Id.* Carter called Mondale his "assistant president." *Id.*

[156] *The Twenty-Fifth Amendment*, 25th Anny. ed., note 9 *supra*, pp. 104-08.

[157] Technically, ratification of Amendments do not become fully effective until the General Services Administration issues a certification of authenticity. GSA certified the 25th Amendment ratification by 38 States on February 23, 1967. Murrill, Brandon J., *The Twenty-Fifth Amendment and Presidential Inability, Part 6: Final Approval and Implementation*, p. 2 CRS Report LLSB11136 (Congressional Research Service, March 28, 2024). As of August 2024, three states —North Dakota, Georgia and South Carolina— have not ratified; they are nonetheless equally entirely subject to the 25th Amendment.

through the 25th Amendment, we have the means of responding to these crises of responsibility.[158]

Amendment Text.

The text of the 25th Amendment as ratified[xlvii] is one of the longest and most complex of the 27 Amendments ratified in the 232 years that began with the first ten—the Bill of Rights—ratified Dec. 15, 1791. It is divided into four sections, the first three of which are simple, each addressing a single problem. Section 4 is long, complex, and seeks to address several knotty problems. Section 1 provides that whenever— and however—the president permanently leaves office, the vice-president automatically succeeds him. Section 2 provides that the new president shall nominate a vice-president, who takes Office upon confirmation by majority vote of both houses of Congress.

Section 3 covers *voluntary* disability.[159] It also specifies implementing procedures: a president who is temporarily disabled must send a written declaration to the Speaker of the House and Senate president *pro tem* advising them of his disability; the vice-president then becomes Acting President. Upon termination of the president's disability, he sends a written declaration of recovery to the Speaker and president *pro tem*. The text of section 3 does not specify when

---

[158] *Id.*, p. 111. For at least the last two years of President Biden's term, we have seen what LBJ called "a vacuum in our national leadership," with no member of the public knowing for sure who has been making critical decisions for the president

[159] During the ratification period, the need for section 3 was made evident by three surgeries LBJ endured under general anesthesia: gall bladder removal (1965); hernia repair and throat polyp removal (1966). Id.

declarations become effective. During George W. Bush 43's first term, Attorney-General Alberto Gonzales was asked by a reporter when voluntary disability declarations become effective. He answered that sec. 3 does not specifically say, and hence (his opinion, not contradicted since) such declarations are effective upon transmittal.[160] But with section 4, declarations of recovery must be *received by* the addressees, in order that they can act within prescribed time limits for responses; the distinction likely rests on the different between a president who voluntarily declares disability, versus one involuntarily removed.[161]

Section 4 encompasses in a single paragraph (numberings below are mine) the thorniest issues surrounding when a president declares, or expresses an intention to declare, himself fit to resume his Office, and designated major players disagree. The "challenge" provisions, covering *involuntary* disability, are necessarily detailed, and can be divided into four parts:

1. Whenever the Vice-President *and* a *majority* of *either* the Cabinet, *or* "such other body as Congress shall by law provide" transmits a written declaration to the Speaker of the House and Senate president *pro tem* that the President

---

[160] *The Twenty-Fifth Amendment*, 3rd ed., note 70 *supra*, p. 202, fn.

[161] During the 1965 Senate Judiciary Committee debate Senator Roman Hruska (R-NE) asked if the House Speaker had gone fishing, would a written declaration have to be delivered to him personally, which would require hunting him down? Senator Ervin (D-SC) answered: "Any reasonable construction would hold that if the President's declaration was written to the office of the Speaker and accepted by his staff there, that this would constitute constructive delivery under normal legal terminology." *One Heartbeat Away*, note 2 *supra*, p. 210.

is unable to discharge the "powers and duties" of his Office,

2. Congress "shall decide" the issue, assembling within 48 hours *for that purpose* if not in session.
3. Sec. 4 declarations become effective when *received*. Within 21 days of such receipt, Congress must decide the issue.
4. If Congress fails to decide, by a *two-thirds vote in each House*, the president *recovers* the "powers and duties" of his Office.

Unspecified in section 4 is whether the declarations therein by the vice-president and by the Cabinet are to be issued jointly or separately. As logistics in emergencies may dictate one form over the other, it was best left unsaid. *Notably, the courts are left entirely out of these matters, with no provision for judicial review.*

One final major omission: if the president-elect or vice-president elect dies after the election and before Congress formally certifies the result. Such a procedure would best be done by another Constitutional amendment. Feerick observes that these kinds of fundamental issues are best decided in periods of relative calm.[162] Thirty years after he made this observation, America is divided in more ways and more deeply than at any time since the Civil War.

Conclusion: If the proverbial best is the enemy of the good, then it can be said that with the 25th Amendment, the perfect is the enemy of the excellent. The 25th covers extraordinarily complex issues with remarkable clarity, few omissions, and wisely leaving unsaid certain matters that are inherently impossible to predict in advance. Put simply, presidential and

---

[162] *The Twenty-Fifth Amendment*, 25th Anny. ed., note 9 *supra*, p. 233.

vice-presidential succession are riven with the uncertainties endemic to countless possible permutations and the vagaries of human fallibility.

Thus, the problems not addressed in 1967 were problems that could not then be addressed. Were the amendment not reported out of Congress, the ratification campaign could not have begun. Looking ahead to the elections of 1968, the 25th Amendment sponsors realized that the results might well bring a new president, changes in key committee assignments and chairmanships, and new members in the House and Senate. The hearings would have had to start over.

The decisions made in 1965 and 1966 triggered the ratification process. Once underway, changes in the White House and Congress due to the 1968 elections could not force starting the hearing process all over again.

As Part IV will show, sections 1, 2 and 3 of the 25th Amendment have all worked very well in practice, for nearly a half-century. Not bad for government work.

PART IV
THE 25TH AMENDMENT IN ACTION
(1973-2024)

The Modern Precedents

Part IV begins with the serial vice-presidential presidential and vacancy crises of 1973-74. The years following saw several assassination attempts (two in 1975 and one in 1981), and multiple instances since of temporary presidential disability, with at first a reluctance to formally invoke the 25th Amendment, and later a better practice of using the 25th to cover instances of temporary disability.

The Succession Crises of 1973-74

What President Nixon's press secretary called a "third-rate burglary" was carried out by seven Republican campaign operatives at an office building in the Watergate Complex[xlviii] on June 17, 1972. By the spring of 1973 it had mushroomed into a first-order campaign finance scandal. The ensuing Senate Watergate Committee hearings[xlix] had by June 1973 of Watergate Summer exposed an amateur-night coverup that was to lead to the president's 1974 resignation. Prelude to the latter had been the 1973 travails[l] of Vice-President Spiro Agnew, who had become a target of a corruption investigation that was to lead to his October 10 resignation. Agnew pleaded *nolo contendere* ("no contest") to a single count of tax fraud, thus avoiding indictment on charges of conspiracy, extortion and bribery, arising out of public contracts awarded during Agnew's tenures as County Executive and Governor.[163]

October 1973 was to prove fateful not only for Agnew but also for Nixon, who on October 20 made the mistake that doomed his presidency, by firing special prosecutor Archibald Cox. When both Attorney-General Elliot Richardson, who had negotiated Agnew's plea deal, and Deputy A-G William

---

[163] *The Twenty-Fifth Amendment*, 3rd ed., note 70 *supra*, pp. 125-34.

Ruckelshaus refused the president's direct order to fire Cox, Nixon ordered Robert Bork, then acting attorney-general, to fire both, thus perpetrating what the press nicknamed the "Saturday Night Massacre[li]." The public outcry forced Nixon to appoint a successor, Texas lawyer Leon Jaworski. Tactically more skillful than law professor Cox; now Nixon faced not an academic, but a savvy trial lawyer, a fateful trade.

October 1973 also saw two tectonic events overseas that could have proven highly destabilizing, had the 25th Amendment not been in place: the Yom Kippur War[lii] and, in its midst, the Arab oil embargo[liii]. The former led to a nuclear alert[liv] for the first time since the Cuban Missile Crisis; the latter triggered the skyrocketing oil prices that caused major recessions in 1973 and 1979, and transferred trillions to sheikdoms, with billions diverted to finance transnational terrorism. Nixon's decision to nominate Gerald Ford, House Minority Leader, was widely praised on both sides of the aisle. Ford's nomination was confirmed in 57 days.[164]

In 1973, a freshman senator, one Joseph Biden, said of Ford's selection:

> [The] *one thing I want to impress upon the American people is that we do not think of this is business as usual, that the man we are going to confirm as the Vice-President of the United States may very well be the next president within the next 3 years.*[165]

---

[164] *Id.*, pp. 135-50. The Senate vote was 92-3 (p. 141), the House vote 387-35 (pp. 149).

[165] *Id.*, p. 135.

Gerald Ford offered reassurance to the senators, as to his plans for 1976: "I have no intention to run, and I can foresee no circumstances where I would change my mind."[166]

Ford was likely sincere, and given the tumult of the times, and first-ever invocation of the 25th Amendment's presidential succession clauses, it was a wise concession to make. As it turned out, in that the powers and perks of the presidency are considerable, Ford came to desire a full term. He was, in the event, unsuccessful. One factor that clearly was negative for some voters was that Ford had ascended without winning an election.

The second succession crisis came in 1974, as impeachment proceedings headed to a climax—Impeachment Summer. The final week of July was to prove the president's Waterloo[lv]. On July 24th in U.S. v. Nixon[lvi] the Supreme Court ruled 8-0 that a president's claim of executive privilege must yield to a subpoena seeking evidence pertaining to a specific criminal case. (Associate Justice William Rehnquist recused himself[lvii], having given legal advice to former attorney-general John Mitchell, regarding Watergate.)

On July 30th, the House Judiciary Committee sent three articles[lviii] of impeachment to the House: obstruction of justice, abuse of presidential power and defiance of a lawful subpoena for taped White House conversations pertinent to the Watergate coverup. Public disclosure of a taped conversation in which Nixon had ordered the FBI director to curtail the Bureau's investigation of certain Watergate matters led a delegation of senior GOP leaders to visit the president. They told him that the full House would surely impeach him,

---

[166] *Id.*, p. 137.

and that enough Republican senators would cross the aisle and vote to convict in the ensuing Senate trial.[167]

On August 8, the president addressed the nation, and announced his resignation, effective August 9. Ford was sworn in, and on August 20 he nominated former New York Gov. Nelson Rockefeller for vice-president. On September 8, Ford pardoned Nixon, who otherwise would have been indicted; the decision angered millions and was a major factor in Ford's losing the 1976 presidential election to Jimmy Carter. On December 9, the Senate voted 90-7 to confirm, and on December 19 the House voted in favor, 287-128. Rockefeller's path from nomination to confirmation took 121 days, more than twice that for Ford.[168]

The late legal scholar and former federal appeals judge, Robert Bork, wrote about a major difference between criminal trials and impeachment, as to the vice-president, compared to that for the president. Art. I, sec. 3[lix] provides, in pertinent part:

> *Judgment in cases of impeachment shall not extend further than to removal from office, and disqualification to hold and enjoy any office of honor, trust or profit under the United States: but the party convicted shall nevertheless be liable and subject to indictment, trial, judgment and punishment, according to law.*

Bork notes that the Constitution is silent as whether a sitting vice-president can be subjected to criminal process. Writing as

---

[167] *Twenty-Fifth Amendment*, 25th Anny. ed., note 9 *supra*, pp. 153-161. As noted earlier, when asked how he felt about being first in line of presidential succession, for a few months in 1973, then-House Speaker Carl Albert answered: *Lord, help me. I pray every night it doesn't happen. Id.*, p. 47.

[168] *Id.*, pp. 167-90. The Senate vote is at p. 183, and the House vote is at p. 184.

to his department's view during his time as acting attorney-general:

> *So, while we had little trouble proving that Agnew did not have an office important enough to necessitate the presidential requirement of impeachment and conviction preceding indictment and trial, we had to take extra care to reaffirm that requirement for the president.*

> *If a president could be indicted and forced to stand trial before being impeached and convicted, he would not officially be incapacitated to the point where the Twenty-Fifth Amendment would apply, but he nevertheless would be effectively removed from heading the executive branch, impermissibly undermining its capacity to perform its constitutionally assigned functions.*

> *The vice president, on the other hand, has very little relevance to governance as a matter of structure and practicality. He becomes relevant only in the event that the president is removed from office, dies, resigns, or becomes incapacitated. Therefore, there is no compelling reason to require that the vice president complete the impeachment process before being indicted.*[169]

Mini-Intervals (1985-2007).

The presidencies of Reagan, George H. W. Bush, Bill Clinton and George W. Bush saw several episodes of routine presidential incapacity due to medical procedures done under general anesthesia. In 1981 Reagan's advisers decided not to formally invoke the 25th Amendment.[170] According to Nancy

---

[169] Bork, Robert H., *Saving Justice: Watergate, the Saturday Night Massacre, and Other Adventures of a Solicitor-General* (Encounter Books, 2013), pp. 64-65.

[170] *The Twenty-Fifth Amendment*, 25th Anny. ed., note 9 <u>supra</u>, pp. xiii-xiv.

Reagan and others, the 25th Amendment was informally invoked when Reagan went under surgery in 1985 for removal of colon polyps; Vice-President Bush was Acting President for eight hours.[171] It was not formally, publicly invoked, for fear that acknowledging presidential disability would alarm the public and our allies.[172] To reassure the world, the first lady stayed at the White House, and the vice-president stayed at his family summer home in Maine. In early 1987, some White House aides reportedly asked chief of staff Howard Baker to evoke the involuntary disability provisions of section 4 of the 25th, asserting that the president was "inattentive and inept." Nothing was done.[173]

In May 1991, President Bush had minor surgery for an irregular heartbeat, but not under general anesthesia, and that December he had an intestinal virus that struck him during dinner during a state visit to Japan; he recovered by morning. In neither instance was the 25th invoked.[174]

During Bill Clinton's presidency, in March 1997 he slipped on stairs while visiting Aussie golfer Greg Norman. The "White Shark" caught Clinton and cushioned his fall, preventing serious injury. The president underwent knee surgery, for

---

[171] *Id.*, p. xvi. At an April 28, 1989, press conference, press secretary Marlin Fitzwater answered a question about the 25th Amendment and vice-president Dan Quayle, in event of disability of the president. Fitzwater referred to Reagan's 1985 cancer surgery episode as an example of prior use of the amendment (sec. 3's voluntary disability provision). *Id.*, pp. xviii-xix.

[172] *Id.*, p. xvi.

[173] *Id.*, p. xviii.

[174] *Id.*, p. xix.

which he was put under local anesthesia. A 25th Amendment letter was drafted, but not transmitted.[175]

George W. Bush and Vice-President Cheney

In June 2002, President Bush formally invoked the temporary disability provisions of section 3 when he was given anesthesia during a colonoscopy. The procedure took only 20 minutes, but Bush did not resume his powers until fully clear of sedation effects. Vice-President Cheney was Acting President for 2 hours, 15 minutes. The ongoing War on Terror[lx] was the stated reason for transferring power. In June 2007 Bush underwent a similar procedure. This time Cheney was Acting President for 2 hours, 5 minutes.[176]

For his part, Cheney, because he had a long history of coronary artery disease, and aware the 25th Amendment does not have a vice-presidential disability provision, had his chief of staff prepare a resignation letter, signed by the vice-president, to be effective upon delivery to the secretary of state[lxi]. Only the president was shown the letter. The president alone would decide whether to deliver the letter.[177]

---

[175] *The Twenty-Fifth Amendment*, 3rd ed., note 70 *supra*, pp. 200-201.

[176] *Id.*, pp. 202-03.

[177] *Id.*, pp 203-04. Only Cheney's counsel and President Bush had copies of the letter. Cheney, who had suffered three heart attacks, made clear to his counsel and his wife that were he stricken suddenly and unable to communicate his wishes, any decision was for President Bush to make. Cheney's counsel kept a copy of the letter at home rather than in the office, for fear that if the White House went into crisis mode he might not be able to retrieve the letter. But his house burned down. He had time to take only two documents, one of which was the vice-president's contingency resignation letter. As Scottish poet Robert Burns famously wrote: "In proving foresight may be in vain: The best laid schemes o' Mice 'an' Men Gang aft agley..."

In Feerick's 1965 article, an important consideration in drafting sections 3 (voluntary declaration of inability) and 4 (involuntary declaration of inability) is that presidents would almost never use section 3, if a challenge might be mounted too his declaration that his voluntary inability had ended; the legislative history of section 3 indicates that its application "should be broadly construed." A challenge would also be used far more often than section 4 involuntary declarations, which inherently invite a challenge to a president's declaration that his inability had ended. Feerick notes that per the legislative history, Congress, in proceeding under Section 4, would have discretion to "request the President to undergo medical tests and examinations, or to submit to questioning at hearings. He cites two historic examples that suggest the president's cabinet would be more likely to act unanimously than alternate bodies, as they are more likely to know the details of a disabled president's condition. The first example is that of James Garfield, where the Cabinet members all recognized that the president was unable to discharge the responsibilities of his Office, yet in the absence of Constitutional warrant to act, stood down. The second case was that of Woodrow Wilson, where the Cabinet officials, though aware of the president's grave disabilities and hence his inability to act, refrained from attempting to sideline the president due to fear that Wilson's lightly regarded vice-president, Thomas Marshall, would then become president.

Donald Trump (2017, 2020, 2021)

Thrice in President Trump's term the idea of using the involuntary disability provisions of section 4 surfaced. In April 2017 Deputy A-G Rod Rosenstein reportedly proposed removing Trump[lxii] because of his firing of FBI Director James Comey, and his alleged collusion with Russia (a claim repudiated by the failure of special counsel Robert Mueller to file any criminal charges against the president). He reportedly gathered evidence by secretly taping the president. Rosenstein denied this, saying his suggestion was "sarcastic" and "in jest."

In October 2020, when both Trump and the First Lady contracted Covid, there was public discussion[lxiii] of presidential disability, if the president's condition worsened, and also, depending upon what medications he was taking. The president rapidly recovered, and nothing came of this.

After the Jan. 6, 2021, Capitol riot, some in Congress called for summarily invoking the 25th Amendment[lxiv]. On Jan. 11 House Speaker Nancy Pelosi give Vice-President Mike Pence 24 hours to invoke the involuntary disability clause of section 4, else she'd call for impeachment. Pence refused. Trump was summarily impeached[lxv] in 24 hours, on January 13. After the inauguration of his successor, he was acquitted[lxvi] on February 13, in his second Senate trial. (Neither the 1998 Clinton impeachment, nor the 2019 first Trump impeachment gave rise to efforts to invoke the 25th Amendment.)

Joseph Biden (2021-2024)

President Biden invoked Section 3 in November, 2021, when he underwent a colonoscopy; vice-president Harris was Acting President for 85 minutes.[lxvii]

In addition to the material cited earlier in the Prologue, there arose a chorus of calls for President Biden to be removed per the 25th Amendment. For reader convenience, here again is the full text of section 4:

Whenever the Vice President and a majority of either the principal officers of the executive departments or of such other body as Congress may by law provide, transmit to the President pro tempore of the Senate and the Speaker of the House of

Representatives their written declaration that the President is unable to discharge the powers and duties of his office, the Vice-President shall immediately assume the powers and duties of the office as Acting President. Thereafter, when the President transmits to the President pro tempore of the Senate and the Speaker of the House of Representatives his written declaration that no inability exists, he shall resume the powers and duties of his office unless the Vice President and a majority of either the principal officers of the executive department or of such other body as Congress may by law provide, transmit within four days to the President pro tempore of the Senate and the Speaker of the House of Representatives their written declaration that the President is unable to discharge the powers and duties of his office. Thereupon Congress shall decide the issue, assembling within forty-eight hours for that purpose if not in session. If the Congress, within twenty-one days after receipt of the latter written declaration, or, if Congress is not in session, within twenty-one days after Congress is required to assemble, determines by two-thirds vote of both Houses that the President is unable to discharge the powers and duties of his office, **the Vice President shall continue to discharge the same as Acting President; otherwise, the President shall resume the powers and duties of his office.** (Emphasis added.)

Given the proximity of events to the upcoming election, this distinction may seem academic. If Biden lives, Harris, who ardently wants to become the first female president, must win the 2024 election to become president-elect, and then be sworn in on January 20, 2025, to become America's 47th President.

Put simply, Section 4 was not designed to forcibly remove a president from office. The Constitution's procedure for such removal is impeachment by the House, per Article I, sec. 2, cl. 5; and then obtaining a conviction at trial in the Senate, per Article I, sec. 3, cl. 6.

To see why this is so, were a vice-president to become Acting President, after a President is sidelined per section 4 of the 25th Amendment—not the case to date with President Biden—she cannot, as some press reports indicate, nominate a new vice-president. Unlike with Members of Congress or the president's Cabinet, a vice-president still holds the office of vice-president, whilst Acting as President when the President is sidelined. Therefore, she cannot nominate a new vice-president. The only way a vice-president can hold the office is by being elected, or selected by a president per section 2 of the 25th Amendment, as happened in 1973 and 1974. Alone among those in the line of presidential succession, the vice-president does not resign her office when she becomes Acting President.

To hold otherwise could create a situation where a President involuntarily sidelined might get well enough to recover the powers and duties of his Office. His return would displace the Acting President. But she could not displace the newly-ensconced vice-president. Indeed NO ONE, not even a sitting president, can bump or fire a sitting vice-president. Nor is there anything in the language or legislative history of the 25th Amendment that support such an interpretation.

The distinction would hardly be academic, if a vice-president became Acting President with years left in the president's term, as there would be a protracted vacancy in the office of the vice-presidency. The last vice-presidential vacancy that lasted over a year was 14 months between Lyndon Johnson's November 22, 1963, ascension to the presidency, and Hubert Humphrey's swearing in as vice-president on January 20, 1965.

This could become a huge vice-presidential succession problem during the current administration, if the president has a stroke and lapses into a coma, unless he has prepared a memorandum to the vice-president akin to that authored by President Eisenhower, on March 3, 1958, which subsequently was adopted by presidents Kennedy and Johnson.

Alternatively, in event of inability of a president to communicate, a properly executed legal instrument (living will, power of attorney) can provide a basis for a surrogate decision on the president's behalf.

Thus, if Constitutional formalities are observed, and absent a legal instrument designating a surrogate decision maker, President Biden will have to agree—or be persuaded to agree—to step down.

Conclusion: Modern 25th Amendment precedents have routinized section 3's voluntary, temporary presidential and vice-presidential disability.

The current presidential succession crisis neither led to the sidelining of the president, nor his resignation. Reports that the president was threatened with removal per section 4 may prove to be accurate, but in fact the 25th Amendment does not empower anyone to forcibly remove a president.

The presidential succession crisis of 2024 exposed the underside of succession struggles, an enduring tension between a reluctance to remove any president, and the desire of a sitting president to remain in office. Neither Constitutional amendment, nor legislative enactment, let alone a clandestine clash between rival factions, can resolve these opposing forces.

PART V
SIX DISABILITY SCENARIOS

Yond Cassius has a lean and hungry look
He thinks too much; such men are dangerous.
William Shakespeare
Julius Caesar, Act I, scene 2.

The Emerging Constitutional Succession Crisis

Six Scenarios

We are in the midst of an emerging—extremely grave—constitutional crisis with the new administration. The America that saw ratification of the 25th Amendment and navigated its way through the acute crises of 1973-1974 was, despite large partisan divisions—inevitable in tumultuous times—at a fundamental, baseline level sufficiently united to survive serial crises intact. There is ample reason to believe we will not be so lucky this time.

The common thread running through all post-25th Amendment events has been the avoidance of deep systemic crises. The broad bipartisan consensus underlying the passage and ratification of the 25th Amendment laid a firm foundation for future orderly transitions. Such a consensus creates lopsided votes in Congress and permits speedy action in a legislature where such is the rare exception; conversely, significant opposition precludes it. Voluntary transitions can be effected in an orderly fashion, as conflict is contained within tolerable bounds. *But an involuntary transition, by its nature, will involve extremes of acrimony and elevated uncertainty.* Its aftermath will be less widely accepted, unless in the end a disabled president's inability to continue is conclusively demonstrated.[178]

---

[178] There is, however, one large difference between President Biden's health status and pre-20th century crises. Medical intervention then was often more likely to do harm than good. Recall that the Father of Our Country was serially bled to death in 1799 by physicians trying—via four such bleedings—draining a total of 32 fl. oz. (two pints)—in two days—to cure the bacterial infection that he contracted working hours in the open field during a steady, soaking rain.

Which brings us to six scenarios. The first three are based on historical antecedents, though two end differently. FOUR includes the long-feared involuntary presidential disability, coupled with a fictive case as presented in a realistic political thriller raising the manifold problems that will likely attend a case of involuntary disability per the 25th Amendment's section 4 "challenge" rules. FIVE has party leaders deciding to force the president out without invoking section 4. SIX departs sharply from historical antecedents of vice-presidential conduct.

To make clear, all six are possible permutations, but none are intended as predictions. The scenarios are intended to paint a picture of what might come to pass—and though clearly drawn with a gimlet eye towards the current crisis, not limited to it, as it might recur, if not in the immediate future, in the distant future. The scenarios are also intended to aid readers conceptually in looking at different types of presidential disability crises.

Scenario One:
President Steps Down
(Near-Antecedent: Dwight Eisenhower 1956-57)

The president's physical and/or mental condition diminishes to the point where he himself realizes that much as he wishes to remain president, he can no longer deceive himself. He steps aside voluntarily—resigns—and the vice-president ascends to the Oval Office.

And as noted earlier, James Garfield died in office, likely due to bad medical care.

Scenario Two:
Protracted, Treatable Disability
(Near-Antecedent: James Garfield 1881)

The president is taken too ill to be able to discharge his obligations. But his illness is easily treatable with modern medicine. For several months he performs few presidential tasks. He recovers and resumes his full pre-illness schedule.

Scenario Three:
Clandestine Regency
(Antecedent: Woodrow Wilson 1919-1921)

The president suffers a massive stroke, unable to discharge any required task at a meaningful level. Nor is there any chance he can meaningfully recover. But instead of using section 3 of the 25th Amendment for a declaration of voluntary disability, or resigning outright, the president hangs on. The First Lady and certain staffers judged loyal by her take over. The vice-president is excluded from this group.

Scenario Four:
Involuntary Sidelining

A president showing signs of mental decline steepens to the point where it is crystal clear to the vast majority of the nation that he cannot continue. Those surrounding him are divided. The First Family wants to stay in power. Top advisers see the ship sinking, as the administration drifts. They decide to press the president's family to help persuade the president to resign. They try, but the president refuses. The vice-president and a simple majority of the Cabinet declare that the president is temporarily unable to discharge the powers and duties of his office. The House and Senate convene; each musters the two-thirds supermajority required for a finding of involuntary presidential disability. The president is sidelined, and the vice-president becomes Acting President, excising the powers and duties of the president, without holding the Office.

This would be **the first-ever** use of the 25th Amendment "challenge" provisions of section 4.

In 1965 the celebrated novelist Fletcher Knebel published a political thriller, *Night of Camp David*. The president goes insane, and a struggle ensues behind the scenes. He invites the freshman senator whom the president wants to run with on his second-term ticket, to spend a weekend night at Camp David. The senator observes the president behaving in ways that lay observers generally consider classic paranoia: a persecution complex ("Everyone is out to get me!") coupled with delusions of grandeur ("A new world confederation of nations, with me as its chosen ruler!"). The senator compares notes with several inside players he knows, and gets moderately positive responses, tempered by skepticism.

Yet doctors apply a more skeptical and nuanced calculus. The young senator fails to convince enough major players—senior members of Congress, and the Cabinet; plus the sitting vice-president, an associate Supreme Court justice and the president's personal physician. He finds *his own sanity* questioned instead. The president learns that the cabal is meeting in a Georgetown townhouse, and interrupts deliberations by surprise. He puts on a bravura performance, confessing to flashes of temper but denies that they collectively equate to insanity.

The game appears over. But at the last moment, before going on television to denounce the cabal, the president learns that his pre-existing heart murmur has become heart tremors. He resigns, and the caretaker sitting vice-president becomes president for the final months. The young senator takes himself out of the running for the nomination. The fall election looms with no incumbent on the presidential ballot.

Scenario Five:
Intra-Party Regicide

The First Family and allied presidential advisers stick together as the president's mental decline accelerates. They aim to accomplish what Woodrow Wilson's triumvirate did: manage the situation as long as they can. Conversely, party leaders decide that the only way to keep the White House come 2025 is to get the incumbent to withdraw from the race. In furtherance, key players leak copiously to friendly Beltway and social media outlets, as to the president's steepening mental decline. The press, fearing that the party they favor will lose both Houses in a mid-term landslide, forces action by boosting public awareness, and fuels public sentiment in favor of replacing the president.

When facing a president reluctant to step down, party leaders have a number of tools at their disposal. All involve carrots, sticks or both. A behind the scenes negotiation will be dictated by the existing relative balance of power between contending factions—too numerous to list in advance, as circumstances will inevitably vary considerably.

Scenario Six
Ride Coattails; Ascend During Second Term

Vice-President Kamala Harris doubts that she cannot win election in her own right if Biden steps aside or is removed. Harris has already made an historical "first": No one in the line of presidential succession has openly declared her capabilities when serving under a president publicly viewed as partially disabled. As noted earlier, Chester Arthur prayed that

Garfield would survive; Thomas Marshall did the same with Woodrow Wilson; John McCormack did so with LBJ; Carl Albert did so with Gerald Ford. Vice-President George H. W. Bush worked at the vice-president's residence during President Reagan's post-shooting 1981 convalescence, so as not to even appear to be angling for the Oval Office.

Yet in an interview with the Wall Street Journal—before the February 8, 2024, release of the special counsel report questioning the president's mental faculties—Harris proclaimed[lxviii]: "I am ready to serve. There's no question about that." She added that everyone who sees her at work "walks away fully aware of my capacity to lead." Such a statement, coming when the president is healthy, is always acceptable. But in the current crisis, it represents the polar opposite of how Bush behaved with Reagan.

Bottom Line. No outsider can truly know in detail the medical condition and prognosis for the current president. He cannot be forced to undergo any medical examination, take any cognitive test, let alone pursue any course of medical treatment. The vast majority of observers are thus limited to the equivalent of searching inside a pitch-dark warehouse with a flashlight emitting a low-wattage flickering beam.

Proponents of the 25th Amendment answered skeptics who raised questions about possible manipulation of procedures formally codified in a Constitutional Amendment by stating that the stability of the republic required its adoption. They recognized that civic virtue was required for presidential succession to work—with or without a new Amendment. Ratifying the 25th Amendment would provide clarity and predictability of presidential and vice-presidential succession to the maximum realistically achievable in 1967.

Going all the way back to the Framers of 1787, our leaders have grasped the essential role of *civita*s. Recall the statements made by senators Bayh and Ervin during the 1965-66 debates on the 25th Amendment, on how in these situations, and in the "white heat" of publicity, our leaders will be spurred to put the public good above personal and political ambitions.

They tried then to answer the famous quip—possibly apocryphal—attributed to Benjamin Franklin[lxix], when asked what the 1787 Grand Convention had produced by spending the summer in Philadelphia behind closed doors: "A republic, if you can keep it."

PART VI
PROTECTING PRESIDENTS AND VICE-PRESIDENTS

Background

As noted earlier, the Secret Service was not tasked with protecting presidents until after the assassination of William McKinley in 1901. Even then, it was not until 1906 that Congress appropriated funds for protecting presidents; the first beneficiary of this was Theodore Roosevelt, who told Henry Cabot Lodge Sr. that his two guards would be "not the least use" against a serious assassin.[179] In 1913 protection was given to presidents-elect, in 1917 to the president's immediate family, and in 1951 to the vice-president.[180] Presidential candidates, if "substantial" and if they did not decline, received protection after the 1968 assassination of RFK.[181]

It took disasters or near disaster to motivate Congress to extend protection. Congress did nothing after the 1958 near murder of Vice-President Nixon in Caracas, who was saved by the Venezuelan police after being trapped for 12 minutes by an angry crowd that pounded on shatterproof glass, tried

---

[179] *Zero Fail*, note 13 *supra*, p. 16. TR called agents "a very small but very necessary thorn in the flesh." *Id.* Presumably he meant this comment to cover threats other than shooting.

[180] Youngblood, Rufus W., *20 Years in the Secret Service: My Life with Five Presidents* (2nd ed., Fideli Publishing, Inc., 2018), p. 15. In 1917, threatening the president was made a federal crime. Kessler, Ronald, *First Family Detail*, pp. 57-58 (Crown Forum, 2014). The law also covers presidents- and vice-presidents-elect, and anyone else in the line of succession to the presidency.

[181] *20 Years in the Secret Service*, note 180 *supra*, p. 188. Congress passed the law unanimously the same day, June 6, that RFK died. Doing the 1968 presidential campaign, the Secret Service racked up more than a quarter-million man-hours protecting candidates. *Id.*, p. 190.

to tip the car over and set it afire.[182] President Kennedy extended full protection to the vice-president in 1962.[183]

Protecting presidents did not become its primary mission until after the JFK assassination, which also persuaded Congress to pass legislation in 1965 making it a federal crime to assault, kidnap, or assassinate a president, vice-president, or conspire to commit or attempt to commit such crimes. The law also covers presidents and vice-presidents elect. Where there is no vice-president or vice-president elect, the law covers the officer next in the line of presidential succession. The law also covers selected members of presidential and vice-presidential staffs.[184]

---

[182] *Id.*, p. 52.

[183] *Id.*, p. 69. This appears to contradict the text and fn. 176., as to how to reconcile decisions made by the Secret Service, and discretion exercised by presidents, as to vice-presidential protection. Agent Youngblood notes that LBJ discontinued protection during his first 14 months as president. *20 Years in the Secret Service*, note 176 *supra*, p. 70. Congress ended this discretionary oscillation for vice-presidential details in the 1965 law it passed.

[184] Title 18 U.S.C. sec. 1751. The law has thrice been amended, in 1982, 1994 and 1996. *Id.* Presidents are entitled to permanent Secret Service Protection per the Former Presidents Act (FPA) of 1958, 3 U.S.C. sec. 102. In 1994 the FPA was amended to limit such protection to ten years, effective Jan. 1, 1997. The Former Presidents Protection Act of 2012 (FPPA) reinstated lifetime presidential protection. Only Richard Nixon has declined protection during his retirement (1974-1994, as of 1985). Presidential surviving spouses are equally entitled per the FPPA, unless they remarry; presidential children are entitled to protection until they turn 16. Vice-presidents are covered by the Former Vice President Protection Act of 2008 (FVPPA), for up to six months after the vice-president leaves office; surviving spouses (unless they remarry) and children up to age 16 are also covered. The secretary of the Department of Homeland Security has discretion to extend additional protection, should circumstances so warrant. Any other protectees can have only temporary protection, per discretion of the Secret Service. The full set of rules for Secret Service protection are codified at 18 U.S.C. sec. 3056.

Protector v. Protectee: Fatal Asymmetries

The central asymmetry presidential protectors face is that given lots of floaters out there who might try to kill a president, would-be assassins need only be successful once; protective details must win every time. In only one confirmed case has a president-elect survived an assassination attempt, only then to be killed after becoming president: JFK, who narrowly escaped death as president-elect.[185]

Protectors face another problem: Their desire to protect the president conflicts with a politician's desire to press the flesh when in public. Facing what promised to be a tight campaign, JFK insisted in his campaign trip to Texas on riding in an uncovered car and repeatedly approaching crowds at the airports and along the motorcade route. He insisted, also, that agents not ride on the back of his car, a position that would have enabled them to shield him—certainly before the final, fatal shot, and possibly even before the first bullet struck the president. Initially, there was confusion; some agents thought the crack was the sound of an exploding firecracker. That delayed a response for critical seconds; agent Clint Hill arrived a split second before the fatal shot struck the president.[186]

JFK had even joked with his agents about getting shot, telling one agent's parents, "I'm sorry for how busy we have been keeping your son. He must be doing a pretty good job, because

---

[185] *Zero Fail*, note 13 *supra*, p. 5-6. The would-be assassin, Richard Pavlick, was an elderly anti-Catholic bigot who had stalked JFK after the 1960 election. He caught up with the family in Palm Beach, and planned to ram his car into Kennedy's as the president was driven to Mass. He balked when he saw JFK's wife and children walking alongside the family car, and was later picked up. *Id.*

[186] Blaine, Gerald, with McCubbin, Lisa, *The Kennedy Detail: JFK's Secret Service Agents Break Their Silence* (Gallery Books, paperback ed., 2011), pp. 212-217.

nobody has shot me yet."[187] In a telling demonstration of the difficulty of stopping shooters in a crowd, the Secret Service ran periodic drills where agents were told who the shooter was in a crowd, yet even knowing that, the agents never were able to prevent the shooter from getting off at least two shots.[188]

JFK understood this, eerily prefiguring how he would die in Dallas, the night before, telling his wife and his close aide, Kenneth O'Donnell:

> *If anybody really wanted to shoot the President of the United States, it would not be a very difficult job—all one would have to do is get on a high building someday with a telescopic rifle, and there is nothing anybody could do to defend against such an attempt.*[189]

Then there is the luck factor: JFK's chosen Secret Service chief, James Rowley, had tallied "50-odd" coincidences on the very day Lincoln was assassinated; had any single one gone the other way, Lincoln would have escaped assassination—that day, at least.[190]

Secret Service historian Carol Leonnig paints a portrait of the agency in 1961. With an annual budget of $5 million, three hundred agents scattered around the country, and only 34 on the White House detail doing eight-hour shifts, it resembled a modest city police force more than a federal agency." Most agents were college graduates from working-class backgrounds, and had either military or police experience—

---

[187] *Zero Fail*, note 13 *supra*, p. 8.

[188] *Id.*, p. 94.

[189] *20 Years in the Secret Service*, note 180 *supra*, p. 122.

[190] *Zero Fail*, note 13 *supra*, p. 51.

indeed, at that time the head of the Service was titled "Chief."[191]

Dallas Flips the Protection Equation: 1963

A final problem, endemic to government, is inter-departmental rivalry. Partly due to disenchantment with the Service, Theodore Roosevelt had created the Federal Bureau of Investigation (FBI) in 1908.[192] The rivalry mattered little, until the dreadful debacle in Dallas. (According to former Secret Service agent J. Lawrence Cunningham, recently the FBI has been criticized for investigating a threat to the president despite the definitive federal statute[lxx] allocating such responsibilities to the Secret Service.)

The Warren Commission Report had scathing comments about the failure of the FBI to share information with the Secret Service—notwithstanding that the Secret Service's own threat criteria did not cover Oswald:

> …*However, there was much material in the hands of the FBI about Oswald: the knowledge of his defection, his arrogance and hostility to the United States, his pro-Castro tendencies, his lies when interrogated by the FBI, his trip to Mexico where he was in contact with Soviet authorities, his presence in the School Book Depository job and its location along the route of the motorcade. All this does*

---

[191] *Id.*, p. 6. As noted elsewhere, agents frequently worked double shifts when protecting protectees during road trips.

[192] *Id.*, p. 63. LBJ wanted the FBI to take over the Service's role entirely. *Id.*, p. 64. Agent Cunningham, who served on the Presidential Protective Detail for 20 years (1974-94), under five presidents (Ford, Carter, Reagan, George H.W. Bush and Clinton), states that the Secret Service-FBI rivalry persists, especially as to investigations during presidential campaign years. Manpower needs for presidential protection divert resources from criminal investigations; over the past 20 years overlapping investigative jurisdictions further exacerbate already-strained inter-agency relations.

seem to amount to enough to have induced an alert agency, such as the FBI, possessed of this information to list Oswald as a potential threat to the safety of the President.[193]

Overall, the Warren Commission's September 1964 report found the agency's protection "seriously deficient" and in need of "significant improvement."[194]

On November 22, security arrangements had been as tight as 1963 technology and the *president* would permit. Clint Hill, who protected Mrs. Kennedy from November 1960 to August 1964, explained that technology available in 1963 did not include magnetometers, video surveillance nor personal communications devices. Agents used hand signals; at airports those let in were known to local police.[195] The presidential limousine at that time was a Lincoln Continental, stretched to accommodate more passengers; it came with three removable tops, all stored in the trunk: hard top, canvas removable top and a transparent Plexiglass bubble top. Hill added that contrary to public opinion, the car was neither armored nor bullet resistant.[196]

As the motorcade proceeded, agents, wearing sunglasses so no one in the crowd can know they are being checked out, were looking for "the glimmer of a gun, or the lone person who is not reacting like the others, but instead has a crazed look in

---

[193] *20 Years in the Secret Service*, note 180 *supra*, pp. 142-43.

[194] *Zero Fail*, note 13 *supra*, p. 68. According to former agent Cunningham, the 300 agents assigned to protect President Kennedy were "woefully inadequate" even by basic protection standards to provide protective services for multiple stops crammed into two days of frenetic activity.

[195] Hill, Clint, with McCubbin, Lisa, *Five Days in November* (Gallery Books, 2013), p. 19.

[196] *Id.*, p. 21.

his eyes, as his hand reaches into his pocket."[197] On November 21, the agents with the president put in 14 hours virtually nonstop, with one flight on Air Force One, one helicopter flight, three short commercial airline flights, rode six motorcades and covered three speech stops.[198]

As motorcades ride, agents routinely perform feats of raw athleticism: In Dallas that fateful Friday, Hill went back and forth between the presidential limousine carrying Mrs. Kennedy, and the backup car immediately behind. This entailed jumping off the side running board of the trailing car, sprinting forward and jumping onto the rear step and grabbing the hand bar affixed to the trunk, all while both cars were moving.[199] When shots rang out, Hill was on the trailing car, usually spaced no more than a couple yards behind the presidential car. He jumped off the running board and dashed for the rear step of the lead car. Hill had to run faster than the lead car, now accelerating to close the gap, nearly 15 mph (15 mph is a four-minute mile pace).[200]

As the lead car accelerated, Hill, whose first attempt to get on the rear step had failed, made a final leap. Had he missed again, the car's acceleration would have thrown the First Lady, who had climbed onto the edge of the trunk, on to the street, and Hill surely would have been run over by the trailing car in less than one second, only a few feet behind and now also

---

[197] *Id.*, p. 25.

[198] *Id.*, p. 60.

[199] *Id.*, p. 93.

[200] *The Kennedy Detail*, note 186 *supra*, pp. 212-14.

accelerating.[201] The driver of the presidential car was also confused by the acoustics of Dealey Plaza, and did not hear the first shot.[202]

For security reasons, JFK's death was not announced until LBJ, driven to Love Field in an unmarked car to avoid attention, was safely aboard Air Force One.[203] LBJ's protective agent, Rufus Youngblood, threw his body over the vice-president as soon as he heard gunshots. He then told LBJ not to go into Parkland Hospital, as he might become Acting President shortly. The agents then rushed LBJ to the airport and on-board Air Force One, partly for security but also because it had a full-fledged communications suite not available anywhere locally.[204]

Recalculating the Equation: 1963-1974

An immediate response to the catastrophe in Dallas was that presidents and other protectees would no longer ride in an open-top car.[205] Chief Rowley took major remedial steps during the Warren Commission's investigation, in essence, trying to deflect the inevitable criticism that would be part of

---

[201] *Five Days in November*, note 195 *supra*, p. 106-08.

[202] *The Kennedy Detail*, note 186 *supra*, p. 355.

[203] *Five Days in November*, note 195 *supra*, p. 116.

[204] *20 Years in the Secret Service*, note 180 *supra*, pp. 88-93. Agent Cunningham recounts that during the flight LBJ asked Youngblood if security protection should be given to the FBI, as had been requested by FBI director J. Edgar Hoover. Eventually, LBJ decided against this.

[205] *The Kennedy Detail*, note 186 *supra*, p. 323. In a supreme irony, the decision not to put the bubble top on the presidential limousine was made mid-morning on the 22nd, as rain showers ended and sunshine emerged in Dallas. *Id.*, pp. 187-88.

the report. He increased White House detail on trips, from 28 to 50; he borrowed FBI agents, pending possible increased funds from Congress; he required more agents to be stationed in crowds, and more scanning of windows along the motorcade route. He contracted with IBM to transition the agency from paper records to automated, computerized systems. And he began a review of all weapons carried by agents.[206]

The first major test of new Secret Service practices came with the 1965 Inauguration. Clint Hill called it the biggest-ever security challenge for the Service. A three-sided bullet-proof glass enclosure was erected to protect the president and vice-president when their oaths were administered.[207] The new presidential limousine sported features that the Service had sought for years: a permanent bulletproof glass roof and windows; titanium plating in the trunk and around the back seat area; a grenade-proof steel floor.[208]

Later that year Congress passed a major reform bill increasing the number of Secret Service agents, appropriating more funds than the Johnson administration had sought, and giving Chief James Rowley the title of Director, to put him on equal level with FBI Director J. Edgar Hoover.[209] A final security upgrade came after a gate crasher drove through the old, rickety front gate of the White House on December 26, 1974;

---

[206] Zero Fail, note 13 *supra*, pp. 60-61. There were 20,000 windows along the Dallas motorcade route. *Killing the President*, note 38 *supra*, p. 121.

[207] Hill, Clint, with McCubbin, Lisa, *Five Presidents: My Extraordinary Journey with Presidents Eisenhower, Kennedy, Johnson, Nixon and Ford* (Gallery Books, 2016), p. 197.

[208] *Id.*, p. 198.

[209] *Id.*, p. 222.

it was replaced by a heavy hydraulic-operated gate, that the Service had long requested.[210]

"Road Trip!": "Agents Away!;" 1959-Present

The era of modern long-range presidential travel began in 1959, when jets supplanted propeller aircraft as the favored mode of air transport. Traveling with protectees entails significant preparations. These are done in three stages. Stage 1 is the *survey*, when agents scope out sites as possible stops; Stage 2 is the *pre-advance*, when detailed arrangements are made in conjunction with local security, police, guards, etc. Stage 3 is the *advance*, when logistics are worked out and specific resources are brought to the site and deployed.[211]

Especially demanding are foreign trips, due to large time zone changes. President Eisenhower embarked on an 11-nation tour in 1959.[212] The trip crossed 10 time zones (GMT-5 to GMT+5), twice in 19 days, covering 22,000 miles.[213] It meant grueling schedules for the agents. One 22-hour day spanned three countries (India, Iran, Greece), with two flights, five motorcades and drew 1.5 million people combined.[214] Securing sites, even with local assistance, could be a daunting

---

[210] *Id.*, p. 419.

[211] Petro, Joseph, with Robinson, Jeffrey, *Standing Next to History: An Agent's Life Inside the Secret Service* (Thomas Dunne Books, 2005), pp. 28-41. Agent Cunningham notes that another factor in evolving security protocols is input from international law enforcement and intelligence agencies.

[212] *Five Presidents*, note 207 *supra*, pp. 23-49. The countries visited: Italy, Turkey, Pakistan, Afghanistan, India, Iran, Greece, Tunisia, France, Spain, and Morocco.

[213] *Id.*, p. 48.

[214] *Id.*, pp. 39-42.

task. In Spain, a dinner was held at the Oriente Palace, the largest palace in Europe. Its 1,450,000 square feet contained 870 windows, 240 balconies and 44 staircases.[215] (By comparison, the White House has 132 rooms, 35 bathrooms, 412 doors, 147 windows, 28 fireplaces, 8 staircases and 3 elevators on six floors.[216])

One problem encountered from time to time when traveling overseas: The locals would refuse outright to use Secret Service personnel, and worse, sometimes insist on having the president ride in an open-top car with the local head of state. When locals in foreign places insisted, the choice was either to scrap the visit, or play by local rules.[217] Overseas, local rules almost always prevailed; at home, the Service usually prevailed.[218]

But not when on foreign territory inside the U.S. The United Nations, as is the case with foreign embassies in the U.S., is not U.S. sovereign territory.[219] Diplomats have diplomatic immunity, and hence can bring guns into the building. Thus, during the 1986 General Assembly Fall session, the U.S

---

[215] *Id.,* p. 47.

[216] *Standing Next to History,* note 211 *supra,* p. 155. The official presidential retreat, originally a U.S. Marine base, was christened <u>Shangri-La</u> by President Franklin Roosevelt in 1942; it was renamed Camp David by President Eisenhower, in honor of his grandson.

[217] *Five Presidents,* note 207 *supra,* pp. 224-228.

[218] *Id.,* p. 377. Agent Cunningham adds that local conventions often play a significant role. Thus, the role of the local sheriff in Germany and France is dual: law enforcement and diplomatic, and frequently their diplomatic role predominates over security concerns.

[219] The UN Headquarters is geographically on U.S. soil, but is governed by an extraterritorial agreement negotiated with the United States.

delegation was to be seated right in front of the Libyan delegation. This would take place shortly after U.S. warplanes had bombed Libya. President Reagan deferred to security concerns, and Vice-President Bush led the U.S. delegation.[220]

A 1967 Vietnam trip almost led to the assassination of Vice-President Humphrey; he was saved by astute Secret Service agents—one of whom, Jerry Parr, later saved President Reagan's life when he was shot in 1981. Humphrey's car had pulled up to a circular driveway at the presidential residence, after President Thieu's inaugural. The other agent decided their car had been waiting too long in one spot, and so he ordered the driver to back up and approach the residence from the other end. Humphrey shouted at the driver: "We can't act like that! That's very arrogant!" A minute later, a

---

[220] *Standing Next to History*, note 211 *supra*, pp. 17-18. Palestinian terrorist leader Yasser Arafat addressed the General Assembly on November 13, 1974, with a gun in his belt. President Ford had ordered Secret Service protection for the 18 hours Arafat would be in New York. Parr, Jerry and Carolyn, *In the Secret Service: The True Story of the Man Who Saved President Reagan's Life* (Tyndale House Publishers, Inc., 2013), pp. 173-74. Parr later learned that on the helicopter trip from JFK Airport to the UN roof, Arafat's terrorist comrades carried grenades that they planned to detonate if the helicopter veered off the planned direct route to the UN. His chief bodyguard was Abu Hassan, a/k/a "the Red Prince." Parr also learned that his real name and rank was Ali Hassan Salameh, chief of operations for Black September, which had perpetrated the massacre of Israelis at the 1972 Munich Olympics. (Israel, which had secretly targeted all the perpetrators, caught up with Salameh in Beirut in 1979, killing him and four associates with a car bomb.) Arafat gave his speech, at the end holding up his gun in one hand, and an olive branch in the other, and warned: "Today I have come bearing an olive branch and a freedom fighter's gun. Do not let the olive branch fall from my hand. I repeat: do not let the olive branch fall from my hand." *Id.*, pp. 170-76. All this said and done around and inside an institution whose credo reads: "They shall beat their swords into plowshares, and their spears into pruning hooks; nation shall not lift sword against nation, neither shall they learn war anymore."

mortar round hit the two vehicles which had been in front of the Vice-President's car. Humphrey apologized.[221]

The toll such trips take on agents and their families is immense.[222]

A Second Reappraisal: 1975-2002

As resources became available, they made possible three-perimeter protection screening: (1) an *outer* perimeter, uniformed police manning barricades, to keep the public at a safe distance; (2) a *middle* perimeter, were agents guard building entranceways and rooftops—including the Service's counter-assault team (CAT) of agents armed with automatic weapons; and (3) an *inner* perimeter, the agents in the president's

---

[221] *Id.*, p. 102. Parr's personal account of the day he saved the president is at pp. 215-238. His account adds details as to just how close a call the president had. Parr noticed, 20 seconds after departing the hotel, that Reagan's blood was oxygenated (red), and wondered if he had punctured the president's lung when he rolled on top of him getting in the car, and fractured one of the president's ribs. Shortly thereafter he rerouted the car to George Washington Hospital. Despite afternoon downtown traffic the driver made to GWH in less than three minutes. Reagan's blood loss was so great that most of the doctors and nurses in the operating room thought he would die. After the crisis had passed, Parr asked Reagan, "Did you know you were an agent of your own destiny?" He told Reagan that as a boy he had seen Code of the Secret Service, a 1939 film that had starred Reagan as Brass Bancroft, an undercover agent in the Secret Service Division of the Treasury Department; four films were made in the series. Reagan replied: "It was one of the cheapest films I ever made!" *Id.*, p. 283.

[222] Parr writes that from 1965 to 1968 it was common for agents, including him, to log over 1,000 hours of overtime annually, much of it unpaid under federal law. *Id.*, p. 96. Clint Hill writes that from December 1966 to December 1967, he was absent from his family 90 percent of the time. *Five Presidents*, note 207 *supra*, p. 242.

Presidential Protection Detail (formerly White House Detail) surround the president.[223]

A signal success for the agents was, as noted earlier, when one agent, Larry Buendorf, was close enough to Lynette "Squeaky" Fromme to thwart her attempt to assassinate President Ford at point-blank range by putting his finger into the chamber, thus preventing the slide from closing.[224] But no amount of agent diligence can protect against a reckless protectee. Late into his presidential term, Jimmy Carter decided to take a riverboat cruise on the Upper Mississippi, making him the first protectee to take such a trip in the 20th century.[225] Carter liked, it seems, to live dangerously:

> *Carter took a lot of chances. Once, impatient with the two minutes it took to lay down the gangplank, he climbed up on the ship's rail and leaped from the boat to the dock. Had he slipped, he'd have fallen maybe thirty feet into the space between. And had he survived the fall, he could have been crushed by the movement of the ship.*[226]

Two years after John Hinckley nearly forced a change of presidents, the Service instituted new protective procedures made possible by new technology: (1) everyone who meets the president in person goes through a magnetometer; (2) everyone in a crowd close to the president is screened; (3) whenever the president travels, a designated "hospital agent"

---

[223] *Standing Next to History*, note 211 *supra*, pp. 18-19.

[224] *Zero Fail*, note 13 *supra*, p. 117. The slide slams forward to lock the gun chamber so it can fire.

[225] *In the Secret Service*, footnote 220 *supra*, pp. 197-201

[226] *Id.*, p. 200.

is stationed on the premises of the primary trauma care facility.[227]

Agents faced heightened threats during the Obama years, four times the prior threat levels, as many as 30 threats per day.[228] The most serious breach of security during the Obama years occurred in September 2014, when a "jumper" clambered over the fence and rushed to the front door, forced his way in and knocked an agent to the floor—having gotten past eight agents starting from a public sidewalk to getting inside the White House in 29 seconds. The jumper got past the agent and made it to the East Room; none of the agents outside came in to help. To make matters worse, agents had seen him in front of the House before, once with a machete.[229] Worse, a few days before the incident, a person armed with a gun had shared an elevator with the president, at the Center for Disease Control in Atlanta.[230]

Upon the formation of the Department of Homeland Security, in 2002, the Secret Service, then with 3,000 agents, was migrated from Treasury to DHS.[231]

---

[227] *Standing Next to History*, note 211 *supra*, p. 141.

[228] *Zero Fail*, note 13 *supra*, p. 285. Former Secret Service agent Dan Bongino notes that the proliferation of social media has led to major threat inflation, as threats are serially passed around online. Bongino, Dan, *Life Inside the Bubble: Why a Top-Rated Secret Service Agent Walked Away From It All* (Post Hill Press, 2020), pp. 100-101.

[229] *Zero Fail*, note 13 *supra*, pp. 387-405.

[230] *Id.*, pp. 405-410. Former agent Cunningham stresses the importance of personal rapport between agents and protectees. Without mutual trust major mistakes are more likely to occur.

[231] *Id.*, p. 248.

On July 13th, 2024, a lone shooter attempted to assassinate former president Trump. Rep. Cory Mills (R-FL), a former Army special ops sniper, stated that the Trump rally should have been relocated to the airport, 15 minutes away and a far more secure area, with no elevated vantage points for assassins.[lxxi]

Proving Mills's point, the Acting Director of the Secret Service told senators at a July 30, 2024 hearing that the agency's failure on July 13 was "A failure of imagination. A failure to imagine that we actually do live in a very dangerous world where people do actually want to do harm to our protectees." He added that the agency assumed that local partners involved in providing security at the event would cover whatever the Service did not cover.[lxxii]

The July 13 assassination attempt that nearly cost former president Trump his life was made possible by epic, astonishing failures by the Secret Service and local authorities. They were of such magnitude that Director Kimberly Cheatle was forced to resign the day after the July 22 House Oversight Committee hearing at which she gave serial evasive answers— essentially, stiffing the Committee and enraging Members of both parties.[lxxiii]

In her July 22 testimony, Cheatle said that her agency's mission is protecting the nation's leaders, and called the agency's performance "the most significant operational failure in decades," yet still gave the agents an "A" grade for July 13.[lxxiv] (Many Members acknowledged that those who put their bodies over Trump after the first shots were fired acted heroically.)

There were many huge failures that day: (a) failure to follow through on a potential threat during the hour prior to the start of the event[lxxv]—one cop saw a "suspicious man" using a range-finder 30 minutes before the shooting[lxxvi]; (b) failure to keep Trump off the stage until a known potential threat was neutralized; (c) failure to hustle Trump away from the site when it was not known if there were additional shooters; (d) failure to secure a landmark local building whose roof gave shooters a direct easy shot for a rifleman; (e) failure of counter-snipers to shoot the rifleman in the 11 seconds before he fired; (f) failure to use drone surveillance as part of the security plan— whereas the shooter used a drone to survey the site[lxxvii]. Indeed, the shooter sent multiple drone flights; he began researching the event upon its announcement on July 3, and registered for the event on July 7.[lxxviii] The shot that took down the would-be assassin was a "million-to-one" shot, as the shooter was sheltered by the roof lip, and only the top of the shooter's forehead and eye behind the gun scope were visible.

A former FBI agent stated that the Secret Service's mission has evolved to be 30 percent protection and 70 percent investigation. Former Rep. Jason Chaffetz, who chaired a 2014 House Oversight Committee investigation of the agency, noted that the average agent in the Uniformed Division received less than 30 minutes of training per year[lxxix]—in 2013, there was no training. The agency is 1,000 agents short, and a recommendation from Obama Homeland Security Secretary Jeh Johnson that the agency hire a director from outside the Service was ignored by the Biden administration.

The lead sharpshooter of Pennsylvania's Beaver County SWAT team stated that the Secret Service did not brief local authorities beforehand.[lxxx] Despite the SWAT team having been on site hours before the rally, a promised morning on-site meeting did not take place.

A prominent cyber-guru reported that off-the-shelf drone technology, already in use by police departments in Florida and South Carolina, would easily have spotted the shooter before he could have unleashed his lethal fusillade at the stage.[lxxxi] Data collected includes manufacturer and model, time and length of activity, flight history and path, and pilot ground location.

At a North Carolina rally in August, 2024, former President Trump requested and got the first ever bulletproof glass shield for any presidential candidate. A Pakistani was arrested July 12 for plotting to carry out an assassination, with the most likely target former president Trump, for his ordering the January 3, 2020 assassination of Qasem Soleimani, commander of Iran's Revolutionary Guard Corps. The would-be assassin planned to complete his mission by the end of August.

Citing death threats, the Secret Service ordered "Dignitary" protection to disgraced former Secret Service Director Kimberly Cheatle. Intended for protection of foreign leaders and lower-profile members of the president's Cabinet, this is a first-ever such use of Secret Service resources to protect an ex-Secret Service chief.

Conclusion: The Secret Service has mostly performed well over the past century, as presidential protection assumed an increasing share of its responsibilities. But in an age of instantaneous pervasive media, threats can materialize from a broader set of sources, and rapidly translate into lethal action. The Secret Service is falling behind. Its failures in 2024 operate as a final warning that major reforms are urgently needed.

PART VII
CONSTITUTIONAL AND
STATUTORY ISSUES

Presidential Succession

CGC Scenario.

The Prologue to this book began with a scenario drawn from the June 2009 report of the Continuity of Government Commission (CGC), in which the president is injured when a commercial jetliner is hijacked and crashes within minutes into the Capitol dome while the president is delivering his State of the Union address. Though the President survives, he is gravely injured. A couple of days later he goes on the air in prime time in an effort to reassure the public; it backfires, as he clearly is not physically or mentally fully capable of resuming his presidency.[232]

The CGC scenario continues. The Secretary of Agriculture at first appears to be the only surviving member of the Cabinet. The Vice-President is dead, as are five Supreme Court Justices and all senators who attended—including the Senate president *pro tem*. If so, he would resign his office and become Acting President. A complication would arise, however, if the Secretary of State were alive, but *incommunicado*. The CGC report suggests that the Secretary of Agriculture would remain Acting President if, subsequently, a higher-ranking Cabinet member turns out to be alive. So, the Secretary hesitates. But after the British prime minister and the Russian president contact him and ask who is President, the Secretary of Agriculture takes the oath of office—but still is only the Acting President.[233]

---

[232] Prologue, p. 3; CGC Second Report, note 5 *supra* (AEI/Brookings, June 2009), pp. 17-24.

[233] *Id.*, pp. 17-19.

Then, at midnight, 50 people buried under the Capitol rubble are discovered. Some are dead, and most of the survivors are badly injured. It is now known that all others in attendance are dead. Besides some staffers, the Speaker of the House is alive, with injuries that are not life-threatening; 19 House members are live, but 15 are in critical condition. Unlike the President, the Speaker is well enough to "bump" the Secretary of Agriculture, and become Acting President, and he does do in the morning. *The nation will have had three presidents—two of them Acting Presidents—within 15 hours.*[234]

Whereas few voters knew who was Secretary of Agriculture, a Gallup poll taken in 2009 (when the scenario takes place) showed that 30 percent of voters could name the Speaker of the House. The 17th Amendment empowers governors to appoint temporary senators until a special election can be held. But there is no such provision for temporary House members. Special elections must be held, and these typically take four months to administer. The Supreme Court cannot reconvene, as by statute a quorum requires at least six, and only four are alive.[235]

The President then transmits his declaration that he is able to return to the Presidency; the Speaker has doubts, but decides to step aside, and as the law requires, resign from the House. The House is now without a Speaker. Later that day, the President meets with the prime minister of Denmark.

---

[234] *Id.*, p. 19.

[235] *Id.*, p. 20. The laws governing House members are in U.S. Constitution, Art. I, sec. 5, cl. 1.2. The quorum rule for the Supreme Court is at 28 U.S.C. sec. 1. Federal trial and appeals courts can function, but do so without the only Court that can resolve differing appeals court rulings.

Suddenly, he collapses and goes into a coma. Though most Constitutional scholars believe the Constitution requires a quorum of 218 members, the four House members disagree, and elect a new Speaker. Further, many Constitutional scholars read the 1947 Presidential Succession Act to permit Acting cabinet secretaries to become Acting President, if they had been already confirmed by the Senate to a lower position in their department.

The military states that it must have a commander-in-chief at all times. So the Undersecretary of State, having won Senate confirmation to that position, and upon learning of the Secretary of State's death in the explosion, becomes Acting Secretary of State, and then—with the Vice-President also dead, and the new Speaker's position of dubious legitimacy due to lack of a House quorum of 218 members—assumes the role of Acting President, per the military's request. He uses a 1794 law[lxxxii] to reconvene Congress at an emergency location if convening in Washington D.C. becomes impossible.[236]

Meanwhile, governors have been appointing temporary senators, and within a few days 90 have convened at Fort McNair, Virginia. (The remaining five states—Alaska, Massachusetts, Oklahoma, Oregon, and Wisconsin—do not allow the governor to make interim appointments, so they must wait months until they hold special senatorial elections.) The 90 senators elect a president *pro tem* not by seniority as an honorific post, but instead pick a Senator who formerly served

---

[236] *Id.*, pp. 22-23. For acts of Congress pertaining to presidential succession, see *Id.*, Appendix II, pp. 59-62. For a detailed exposition or emergency laws, see *National Emergency Powers*, Congressional Research Service (CRS) report 98-505 (Feb. 27, 2019).

as Secretary of State. Upon taking office, he immediately bumps the Acting President—who had been undersecretary of state, then Acting Secretary of State. This happens because the Senate president *pro tem* is in the statutory line of succession, whereas Acting Secretaries *are not listed in the 1947 succession law*.[237]

Until the House can get a quorum of 218 members, it cannot act. Without a bicameral legislature, there can be no legislation, no declarations of war, and no appropriations. The nation is paralyzed for months.[238]

CGC Assessment

Debates center on three issues: (1) While there is general agreement that if a temporary vacancy exists in the Presidency, the Vice-President becomes Acting President, until the Presidential disability ends, proposals for new legislation remained unresolved; (2) To whom does "Officer" apply? On one side, those who see the capital "O" interpret it as applying only to officers in the executive branch; those who oppose this hold that legislative officers can ascend to become Acting President; (3) In event of a double vacancy, Congress can provide by law for special elections. Again, the dispute centers on whether the term includes legislative officers.[239]

---

[237] CGC Fourth Report, note 7 *supra* (AEI/Brookings, December 2022), pp. 23-26.

[238] CGC Second Report, note 5 *supra*, pp. 23-24.

[239] *Id.*, p. 26.

1792 Succession Law

The Senate president *pro tem* and the House Speaker, in that order, were the only persons who could become Acting President. During the period 1792-1886, four presidents and five vice-presidents died in office; the vice-presidency was vacant one-quarter of the time, including a seven-year stretch in which there was a vice-president for one month.[240]

1886 Succession Law

Congress removed legislative officers from the line of succession and replaced them with the seven members of the Cabinet, in the order that the departments were created. Cabinet members had to have been confirmed by the Senate, not be under impeachment and meet all three Constitutional requirements for presidents (natural citizen at birth, resident in the U.S. for at least 14 years, and at least 35 years of age).[241]

1947 Succession Law

At Truman's insistence, the legislative leaders were put back in the line of succession, with the House Speaker first, as the Speaker is elected by the people; the Senate president *pro tem* was second, in that senators pick from among their colleagues who gets the office.[242] This came at a time when partisan divisions were much narrower than they are today. The CGC

---

[240] *Id.*, p. 27.

[241] *Id.*, pp. 30-32. The order of succession was State, War, Treasury, Attorney-General, Postmaster General, Secretary of the Navy and Secretary of the Interior.

[242] *Id.*, 32-33.

report highlights problems that need fixing. Most important are the presence of legislative officers in the line of succession, so-called "bumping" procedures; and keeping the line of Cabinet succession in the order the departments were created.[243]

CDC Key Recommendations

There are three overriding priorities: (1) move some of those in the line of succession to live and work outside of Washington, D.C.; (2) take legislators out of the line of succession; (3) change the order of Cabinet officials in the line of succession.[244]

Presidential Succession Update

In December 2022, the CGC issued its final report on presidential succession.[245] It was reconvened in the aftermath of the Covid pandemic.[246] It made one Core Recommendation: Remove Congressional leaders from the line of succession. It also made four Additional Recommendations: (1) Clarify in law that Acting Secretaries of Departments are not in the line of succession; (2) Clarify the process surrounding the incapacitation of the Vice-President—especially in event of a double vacancy or protracted incapacity of President and Vice-President; (3) Provide in law for Presidential succession if both the winning

---

[243] *Id.*, pp. 39-44.

[244] *Id.*, pp. 45-49.

[245] CGC Fourth Report, note 7 *supra* (AEI, Dec. 2022) (CGC Fourth Report).

[246] *Id.*, p. 3.

President and Vice-President die before Inauguration Day; (4) Address the electoral counting process so that there is no Presidential vacancy on Inauguration Day.[247]

In service of the above, the CGC presented three scenarios for the transition period between the election and the inauguration: (1) the winning candidates die after Election Day and before the December Electoral College voting; (2) the winning candidates die after the Electoral Vote (EV) count in December and before the Congress convenes in January to certify the EV count; (3) the winning candidates die after Congress certifies the EV count in January and before the January 20 Inauguration Day.[248]

Towards those ends, the CGC recommends that there be a 20 percent threshold for objecting to an EV slate, to be reached in both the House and the Senate; that no competing slates be sent to Congress; and that in the end the chosen replacements for the deceased candidates both be from the same political party.[249]

---

[247] *Id.*, pp. 4-5. A detailed, granular examination of the myriad options attending these measures is beyond the scope of this book.

[248] *Id.*, pp. 10-11.

[249] *Id.*, pp. 16-18.

PART VIII
SUCCESSION IN
MASS CASUALTY EVENTS

Continuity of Congress

Because presidents cannot govern by executive fiat, a mass casualty event that destroys the ability of Congress to operate makes Constitutional governance impossible. On September 11, 2001, American Airlines Flight 77 took off from Reagan National Airport, made a U-turn near Cleveland and headed back to Washington D.C., its transponder off, at 500 mph—a mile every seven seconds. Heading directly towards the White House, it swerved at the last minute and slammed into the Pentagon.

Vice-President Cheney was rushed from his office by Secret Service agents, down to the White House bunker, only to discover that the agents did not have the military security key needed to open the door. So, they all waited at the foot of the stairs. Had Flight 77 hit the White House, the vice-president's survival chances were slim.[250]

Meanwhile United Flight 93 had taken[lxxxiii] off from Newark International Airport, headed for San Francisco. The other three flights, two originating from Boston and one from Washington-Reagan National Airport, were supposed to fly to Los Angeles. Flying transcontinental routes meant the planes would carry full fuel loads. But 46 minutes into United Flight 93's journey, the flight, then over Pennsylvania, suddenly turned back towards Washington D.C. Because the plane had taken off 41 minutes late, in-flight passengers had heard from family and friends that they were headed back to Washington, D.C. as part of a terrorist attack. Led by hero for the ages Todd Beamer, passengers stormed the cockpit, and the pilot

---

[250] *Zero Fail*, note 13 *supra*, pp. 225-244.

put the plane in a steep dive, crashing into the Pennsylvania countryside. Had the plane taken off on time, it would have hit the Capitol building. Few members were present— although one member present was the Speaker of the House.[251] That the plane was headed for the Capitol was confirmed by two al-Qaeda 9/11 masterminds in a September 8, 2002, interview on Al-Jazeera.[252]

CGC N-Scenario

It is 11 AM on Inauguration Day. The president and top aides and Cabinet nominees are meeting at the White House; leading members of Congress and most other members in both parties, the justices of the Supreme Court, families and friends await the presidential party in front of the west side of the Capitol. A nationwide television audience is watching (as well as millions more around the globe). The screens go blank. A small al-Qaeda nuclear device has been detonated midway between the Capitol and the White House. Everything within a one-mile radius is destroyed. Everyone within that radius is presumed dead. There are no president- or vice-president elect, no justices, no Congressional leadership. *Who governs? Nobody knows.*[253]

The CGC scenario suggests that if Congress is obliterated, likely unilateral executive action would be implemented— "perhaps a benign form of martial law."[254] As the minutiae of

---

[251] CGC First Report, note 4 *supra*, p. 2.

[252] *Id.*, Appendix II, p. 34.

[253] *Id.*, note 4 *supra*, p. 1.

[254] *Id.*, note 4 *supra*, p. 4.

Congressional procedure lie well outside the scope of presidential succession, I raise only a few points made by CGC.

During the years 1947-1965, more than thirty proposed Constitutional Amendments dealing with mass vacancies were proposed, but only three came to a vote. These three proposed Constitutional Amendments were passed by huge margins in the Senate. The House took no action on the first two, and partial action on the third. In 1954, Senator William Knowland (R-CA) proposed an Amendment that would allow state governors to appoint temporary House members when more than 145 House seats were vacant; it passed the Senate 70-1, but the House did nothing. In 1955 Senator Estes Kefauver (D-TN) introduced an Amendment providing for gubernatorial appointments of temporary House members when a majority of House seats were vacant; it passed the Senate 76-3 but died in the House. In 1960 the Senate passed a three-part Constitutional Amendment by a vote of 70-18. Two parts passed the House: one part became the 23rd Amendment[lxxxiv], giving D.C. voters the right to vote in federal elections; another part became the 24th Amendment[lxxxv], abolishing the poll tax. The House ignored the third part, about filling mass vacancies.[255]

A special case is an attack that kills mostly members of one party in key states. This could lead to a new Congress radically different from the previous one. A Democratic governor could appoint 52 Democrats to fill the delegation seats. Conversely, if an attack kills the Texas delegation, a Republican governor could fill all 38 seats. (I use 2020

---

[255] *Id.*, p. 17.

redistricting figures[lxxxvi] instead of the 2000 figures used in the CGC report).[256] *The CGC strongly recommends that any Constitutional Amendment proposed require ratification not in the seven years typical of recent ratified Amendments, but in two years, due to the extreme nature of the threat.*[257]

The CGC updated its May 2003 report on Continuity of Congress in April 2022. In pursuing its aims of getting a Constitutional amendment to allow governors to make temporary appointments, pending the results of special elections, the CGC made three specific recommendations: (1) create a limited provision to allow members to use remote access when not in Washington, D.C.; (2) allow temporary replacement members when deceased plus incapacitated members are a majority; (3) adopt measures to allow Congress to convene remotely, if access to the Capitol is precluded (after a mass casualty event).[258]

Two new recommendations merit special attention: Each member of the House should submit a list of designated successors, in event the member dies or is incapacitated.[259] And: Repeal House Rule XX, clause 5 of which provides for a very small number of members making a quorum; the CGC believes this rule unconstitutional and unwise.[260]

---

[256] *Id.*, p. 23.

[257] *Id.*, p. 30.

[258] CGC Third Report, note 6 *supra*, p. 1.

[259] *Id.*, p. 3.

[260] *Id.*, pp. 3-4.

Conclusion: The central objective of the CGC was to create rules that prevent a partisan shift of governance in the aftermath of a mass casualty event. A second objective was to establish minimum levels of Congress to make governance acceptable to the public. A final goal was to create the institutional and technological capability to enable remote governance if Washington, D.C. is destroyed by a terror attack or incapacitated by a pandemic.

PART IX
AUTHOR'S CONCLUSIONS
AND RECOMMENDATIONS

Next: A Replay of 1886?

What would work best is to once again remove Congress from the succession line, as was done in 1886. But the stars do not seem aligned for this to happen. The current line[lxxxvii] of Cabinet succession runs to 15 of its 16 members, as Homeland Security Secretary Alejandro Mayorkas is foreign-born, and hence ineligible.

Proposals since 1886 have included limiting the Cabinet succession line to a few department heads likely to possess national security experience—with State and Defense the first two in line, typically followed by Treasury (currently between State and Defense in the line). The problem with this is that there have been secretaries of other departments more knowledgeable than those ahead of them. The classic example of James Schlesinger comes to mind. Before being chosen as America's first Energy Secretary by Jimmy Carter, he had been chairman of the Atomic Energy Commission and CIA Director under Richard Nixon, and Secretary of Defense under Gerald Ford. As head of the 13th executive department created, he stood last in the line of succession. The sole secretary ahead of him, with meaningful national security credentials, was Defense Secretary Harold Brown.

Further, while secretaries of state are generally regarded as qualified, Treasury secretaries include people with no national security credentials to speak of. Salient examples at Treasury—generally chosen for financial or economic expertise—include Paul O'Neill under George W. Bush and Timothy Geithner under Barack Obama. Conversely, one of Richard Nixon's Treasury secretaries was George Shultz, who later was one of Ronald Reagan's secretaries of state; Bill Clinton, with no national security background, chose

Democrat Lloyd Bentsen for Treasury, who also had deep national security experience.

Presidential and Vice-Presidential Disability Declarations. The President. & VP should be required by law to file with the House and Senate disability declarations akin to President. Eisenhower's March 3, 1958, memo, appointing proxies with full legal power of attorney to declare such inability, if they are unable to act.

A Cabinet Succession Reboot. Simply removing the House Speaker and Senate president *pro tem* is a step in the right direction. But revising by statute how the order of Cabinet succession works can further improve the presidential succession equation.

Specifically:

1. Each new president should start—whether at the start of a four-year term, or after a presidential term curtailed by death, illness, resignation, or removal—with the default list ordered by time of departmental creation. (This allows all presidents, however they ascend, to start with the same default list, not influenced by a predecessor's choices.)
2. At any time, the president may re-order the line of succession, as to how they should be ranked in terms of fitness to become president. (This judgment would of course factor in lots of issue expertise besides national security, as well as executive ability and character.)
3. The president's list then would be submitted to both Houses of Congress. Congress would have 10 calendar days to vote on the list up or down, exactly as sent, *i.e.*, without alteration. This ensures that there can be neither "legislative day" maneuvers, nor negotiation as to

shuffling of the president's preferred Cabinet succession deck.

4. Unless *both* Houses, by a two-thirds supermajority, vote to *reject* the entire list, the president's choice prevails. This means a clearly bipartisan vote will be required to reject the list.

Key Mass Casualty Measures. The first three sections of the 25th Amendment have worked extremely well, enabling multiple orderly transitions during the turbulent Watergate years of 1973-74. But there is a huge growing gap between the possibility of mass casualty events and the inability of current arrangements to cope with mega-catastrophe. The recent pandemic and destructive lockdowns affected nearly every country, and hence adversaries could not exploit America's near paralysis; they, too, were paralyzed. This likely will not be the case in event of a surprise attack.

The Continuity of Government Commission offered a number of constructive suggestions for coping after mass casualties[261]:

1. Remove Congressional leaders from the line of presidential succession. If Congress insists on staying in, make sure the successors are from the same political party as were the president and vice-president.
2. House members should designate several temporary successors in event of their death or incapacity, to serve until special elections can be held. A baseline requirement for triggering this—*e.g.*, loss of one quarter or one third or one half of members—should be set.

---

[261] *Id.*, pp. 5-9.

3. Establish remote network access to connect all members of Congress, in the event Washington becomes bio-hazardous or is destroyed.

Complicating recovery is the extreme partisanship that has emerged in today's politics. Writing in 2022, law professor Joel Goldstein noted that in 37 of the past 53 years, the president and Speaker were from opposing parties. During the first three quarters of the 19th century, the president and Senate president *pro tem* had almost always been members of the same party; but from 1879 to 1885, three of four Congresses featured a Senate controlled by the opposition party. Informing Truman's reinsertion of Congress into the presidential succession law, and putting the House Speaker first, was that from 1898 to 1945, the president and House majority were from the same party nearly 90 percent of the time.[262]

A second complication is the issue of martial law. The CGC suggested that in event of a mass catastrophe, the surviving government might impose "a benign form of martial law." Historically, martial law has been a rarity in America. The first documented instance was in 1814 when Andrew Jackson did so upon defeating the British in the Battle of New Orleans. Next came martial law imposed on the defeated Confederacy by Union military leaders. Martial law was imposed a few times in the 20th century: to quell labor or race riots; during World War II on the Territory of Hawaii for three years after Pearl Harbor, and upon Japanese-Americans during their wartime

---

[262] Goldstein, Joel K., *History of the Legislative Succession Provisions in the Presidential Succession Act of 1947*, vol. 91, Fordham Law Review 13, 17 (2022).

internment; and to enforce racial desegregation in the 1950s and 1960s.[263]

Yet in 1962, at the height of the Cold War and under threat of nuclear annihilation, the Kennedy administration took the position that even after a nuclear strike on U.S. soil, "nationwide martial law is not an acceptable planning assumption."[264] It would be a "bet the company" wager that after a mass casualty event in our current political and social environment, similar restraint to that shown by the Kennedy administration would be exercised.

Reform the Secret Service

The Service[lxxxviii] has found its personnel, equipment and budgetary priorities rarely met, due to being a small fish in the big pond of two large bureaucracies, first Treasury, and now the Department of Homeland Security. Suggestions:

1. Establish the Secret Service as an independent agency—the Secret Service Bureau (SSB) and move it outside of Homeland Security's ultra-bloated bureaucracy. This would allow the SSB to lobby effectively for its budget size and composition. The present arrangement has the Service's priorities subordinated to more powerful agencies in DHS.
2. Make the sole SSB mission protecting presidents and other officials, families, etc., including foreign dignitaries;

---

263 Relyea, Harold C, *Martial Law and National Emergency*, CRS Report for Congress (Congressional Research Service, Jan. 7, 2005).

264 *Id.* There are in place a number of National Emergency laws that might be invoked. *National Emergency Powers* (Congressional Research Service, Report 98-505, Feb. 27, 2019).

SSB would maintain liaison relationships with other agencies—FBI, CIA, etc., on selected issues.[265]

---

[265] The Service's protection function has expanded several times since its formation, most recently in 1998, per Presidential Decision Directive 62 (PDD 62), when it was tasked with providing security for National Special Security Events (NSSEs). In 2024, both the Republican and Independent presidential campaigns were unable to get the Secret Service to provide traditional protections to their respective candidates. The GOP sought a three-mile security zone around their Convention site in Milwaukee, similar to that for the Democratic Convention in Chicago; but the Service initially would only provide a quarter-mile security zone for the GOP. Moran, Rick, Secret Service Won't Budge in Moving Security Zone Further from GOP Convention in Milwaukee (PJ Media, May 11, 2024). Four weeks later, the Service was reportedly reconsidering the size of the zone; it purportedly sought to balance security for the attendees versus the right of protesters to exercise their First Amendment rights. Milwaukee police, to whom the Service initially delegated security decisions, said that the real security threat is disruptions caused by Convention delegates. Moran, Rick, Secret Service may be *Backing Off Plans for Unacceptable 'First Amendment Zone' at Milwaukee Convention* (PJM, June 8, 2024). At a June 21 joint press conference, the Republican National Committee and the City of Milwaukee disclosed the final security arrangements for the GOP Convention. The arrangements are very detailed, but distances are not specified. Clearly, the protest zones are farther away then what the city originally offered. The Biden administration turned down a request from Robert F. Kennedy Jr. for Secret Service protection. This was the first-ever candidate request that any administration has denied since protection was extended to presidential candidates 55 years ago. While the normal practice has been to give major candidates protection starting 120 days before November, Jimmy Carter gave Edward Kennedy protection 441 days before the November 1980 election, when Kennedy had not even formally declared his candidacy. Ronald Reagan extended protection to Jesse Jackson 362 days before the 1984 election, and 351 days before the 1988 election. Donald Trump provided protection to Joe Biden 231 days before the 2020 election. Louderback, Jeff, RFK Jr. Says Kennedy Siblings Asked Biden to Give Him Secret Service Protection (NTD, April 28, 2024). After the July 13, 2024, attempt to kill former president Trump, the Secret Service extended protection to RFK.

3. Detach non-germane parts. *Why is the Secret Service providing community outreach and childhood safety?* [266] This would reduce the SSB's budgetary requirement.
4. Expand budget to fully fund SSB agent rosters and other resources.[267]
5. Adopt commercial airline-pilot hourly limits for on-duty service, with exceptions only to address sudden, extreme emergencies.
6. Update the SSB suite of technology across the board.
7. Require annual breaks for supplemental training and capability re-qualification.

Former agent Cunningham, who served under three directors during his 20-year tenure, said that all three lamented the difficulty in competing for funding increases.[268] Congress was only willing to do so given an expanse in agency jurisdiction. Further, protection-related expenses are highly sensitive to sudden changes in demand for services; sudden events may require a steep increase in resources already stretched to the limit.

---

[266] *United States Secret Service Annual Report*, p. 25, FY 2023. For the Service's Year in Review; see *Id.*, pp 10-13.

[267] The Secret Service FY 2023 budget was $2.822 billion.

[268] In the two years preceding the JFK assassination, three Service chiefs pleaded for more agents, believing that a few dozen could have made a difference in security. Their requests were greeted with scorn. Republican members asked if the added funds would pay for Caroline Kennedy's ponies. Iowa GOP Rep. Harold Gross asked, having seen a photo of a Secret Service agent driving a boat as Mrs. Kennedy water-skied, "Do you suppose I could get some Secret Service men to tow me around if I wanted to water-ski?" *Zero Fail*, note 13 *supra*, p. 51.

What makes today's partisanship so dangerous and obstructive is that the divide is not simply over policy. *It is over the very structure of government and the balance between governmental power and individual rights*—with rising claims of selective group rights for currently favored constituencies.

Give the Executive and Judicial Branches Co-Equal Protection Status

Congress has "seat of government" protection—the Capitol Police protect the Capitol building, and can be called in by the Speaker of the House and Senate Majority Leader. D.C.'s local government offers supplemental police protection, as it did on January 6, 2021. But aside from the Secret Service, there was little protection at the White House when in 2020 rioters stormed the White House and; tried to break down the fence; this led Secret Service agents to rush President Trump, the First Lady and their son, Barron, to a secure room inside the White House.[269] *Just as the Capitol is the seat of government for the Legislative Branch, so is the White House for the Executive Branch.* Any president should have the same ability to call on resources, including the National Guard, without needing approval of the local authorities.

Similarly, the Supreme Court building is the seat of government for the Judicial Branch.[270] After the June 2022 arrest of a would-be assassin near the home of Justice Brett Kavanaugh, President

---

[269] Rambaran, Verdana, at least 60 Secret Service members injured during George Floyd protests in D.C. *(Fox News, May 31, 2020). Collins, Kaitlan and Gray, Noah,* Trump briefly taken to underground bunker during Friday's White House protests *(CNN, June 1, 2020).*

[270] See paragraphs in Part II, The Assassin's Veto, assassination attempt on Justice Kavanaugh.

Biden signed the Supreme Court Police Parity Act of 2022[lxxxix], extending protection to the Justices and their families. *Such tripartite protection and security is consonant with the Constitution's creation of three co-equal branches.*

Changes in 1967 reflected overwhelming consensus as to the need for something to be done. Such consensus has been shattered. Current presidential succession statutory laws are a ticking time bomb, accidents waiting to happen. The state of near open civil war that prevails today between the political parties and within the electorate virtually precludes bipartisan cooperation. It likely will take electoral outcomes that significantly alter the balance of power, to make possible revision of existing presidential succession laws. Or, as happened after the Kennedy assassination, and the unsuccessful attempts on the lives of Ford and Reagan, changes might be forced by what the late exiled Soviet dissident Alexander Solzhenitsyn called[xc] in 1978 "the pitiless crowbar of events."

Closing Note

Crises present challenges, but also offer opportunities. The 1962 Cuban Missile Crisis brought America and the former Soviet Union to the brink of nuclear holocaust; the first response was the Hot Line, enabling rapid communication before crisis becomes war. The 2024 presidential succession crisis exposed a growing risk to societal stability; adopting reforms can reduce the likelihood and severity of future succession crises. Central to such an inquiry will be recalling the wisdom of the 25th Amendment Framers: They accepted the limits of what was achievable in 1965 (the year that the Amendment was passed by Congress, enabling the ratification process to begin). Back then, removing the House Speaker and Senate president pro tem was taken off the table, due to adamant opposition in Congress. Opportunities to address problems left unresolved then now arise from the half-century of experience we have with the Amendment in action. Sections 1, 2 and 3 are working smoothly, so nothing more need be done. President Biden's term exposed the raw underside of Section 4's involuntary disability declarations: they will, in reality, never be fully resolvable.

APPENDIX 1
CHESTER ARTHUR
LIST OF SUCCESSION ISSUES

In his 1881 message to Congress, President Arthur raised eight sets of succession issues that needed to be addressed.

As indicated in the text, none of these were addressed until 1967, when some were dealt with. Others remain unresolved. The eight sets may be divided into those pertaining to determining presidential disability, those pertaining to the power exercised by the vice-president when a president is sidelined by disability, and duration of their exercise thereto.

Below are Arthur's points, with notations on the status of each today.

Presidential Disability

Is the inability limited in its nature to long-term intellectual capacity, or has it a broader import? What must be its extent and duration? How must its existence be established? **Partly resolved by 25th A., sec. 4.**

Has the President whose inability is the subject of inquiry any voice determining whether or not it exists, or is the decision of that momentous and delicate question confided to the Vice-President, or is it contemplated by the Constitution that Congress should provide by law precisely what should constitute inability, and how and by what tribunal or authority it should be ascertained? **Partly resolved by 25th A., sec. 4.**

Apportionment of Powers Between President and Vice-President

If the inability proves to be temporary in nature, and during its continuance the Vice-President lawfully exercises the functions of the

Executive, by what tenure does he hold his office? **Resolved by 25th A., sec. 3: the vice-president serves as Acting President.**

Does he continue as President for the remainder of the four years' term? Or would the elected President, if his inability should cease in the interval, be empowered to resume his office? **Resolved by 25th A., sec. 4.**

And, if, having such lawful authority, he should exercise it, would the Vice-President be thereupon empowered to resume his duties as such? **Resolved by 25th A., secs. 3 & 4.**

BIBLIOGRAPHY

Books

Bayh, Birch, *One Heartbeat Away: Presidential Disability and Succession* (1968)

Blaine, Gerald, and McCubbin, Lisa, *The Kennedy Detail: JFK's Agents Break Their Silence* (Gallery Books, 2010)

Bongino, Dan, *Life Inside the Bubble: Why a Top-Ranked Secret Service Agent Walked Away From It All* (Post-Hill Press, 2020)

Bonnie, Richard S., Jeffries, Jr., John C., Low, Peter W., *A Case Study in the Insanity Defense: The Trial of John W. Hinckley, Jr.* (Foundation Press, 4th. ed., 2021)

Bork, Robert H., *Saving Justice: Watergate, the Saturday Night Massacre, and Other Adventures of a Solicitor General* (Encounter Books, 2013)

Craughwell, Thomas J., *Stealing Lincoln's Body* (Belknap Press, 2007)

Feerick, John, *From Failing Hands: the Story of Presidential Succession* (Fordham Univ. Press, 1965);

Feerick, John, *The Twenty-Fifth Amendment: Its Complete History and Applications* (25th Anniversary ed, Fordham Univ. Press,1992)

Feerick, John, *The Twenty-Fifth Amendment: Its Complete History and Applications* (3rd ed., Fordham Univ. Press, 2014)

Feerick, John, *That Further Shore: A Memoir of Irish Roots and American Promise* (Fordham Univ. Press, 2020)

Events in Telecommunications History (AT&T Historical Archives ed., 1992)

Greenberger, Scott S., *The Unexpected President: The Life and Times of Chester A. Arthur* (Da Capo Press, 2017)

Heckscher, August, *Woodrow Wilson* (Collier Books, Macmillan Publishing Company, 1991)

Helferich, Gerald, *Theodore Roosevelt and the Assassin: Madness, Vengeance, and the Campaign of 1912* (Lyons Press, 2013)

Hill, Clint & McCubbin, Lisa, *Five Days in November* (Gallery Books, 2013)

Hill, Clint w. McCubbin, Lisa, *Five Presidents: My Extraordinary Journey with Eisenhower, Kennedy, Johnson, Nixon and Ford* (Gallery Books, 2016)

Holzer, Harold, *President Lincoln Assassinated!! The Firsthand Story of the Murder, Manhunt, Trial, and Mourning* (Special Publication, Library of America, 2014)

Jeffers, H. Paul, *An Honest President: The Life and Presidencies of Grover Cleveland* (William Morrow, 2000)

Kauffman, Michael W., *American Brutus: John Wilkes Booth and the Lincoln Conspiracies* (Random House Trade Paperback ed., 2005)

Kessler, Ronald, *The First Family Detail: Secret Service Agents Reveal the Hidden Lives of the Presidents* (Crown Forum, 2015)

Knebel, Fletcher, *Night of Camp David* (Harper Collins, 1965)

Leonnig, Carol, *Zero Fail: The Rise and Fall of the Secret Service* (Random House, 2021)

McCullough, David, *Truman* (Simon & Schuster, 1992)

Millard, Candice, *Destiny of the Republic: A Tale of Madness, Medicine, and the Murder of a President* (Doubleday, 2011)

Miller, Nathan, *FDR: An Intimate History* (Madison Books, 1983)

Miller, Scott, *The President and the Assassin: McKinley, Terror and Empire at the Dawn of the American Century* (Random House Trade Paperbacks, 2011)

Oliver, Willam M. & Marion, Nancy E., *Killing the President: Assassinations, Attempts, and Rumored Attempts on U.S. Commanders-in-Chief* (Praeger, 2010)

Parr, Jerry & Carolyn, *In the Secret Service: The True Story of the Man Who Saved President Reagan's Life* (Tyndall House Publishers, Inc., 2013)

Petro, Joseph (w. Jeffrey Robinson), *Standing Next to History: An Agent's Life Inside the Secret Service* (Thomas Dunne Books, 2005)

Picchi, Blaise, *The Five Weeks of Guiseppe Zangara: The Man Who Would Assassinate FDR* (Academy Chicago Publishers, 1998)

Posner, Gerald, *Case Closed: Lee Harvey Oswald and the Assassination of JFK* (Random House, 1993)

Rehnquist, William H., *Grand Inquests: The Historic Impeachments of Justice Samuel Chase and President Andrew Johnson* (William Morrow & Co., Inc., 1992)

Rosenberg, Charles E., *The Trial of the Assassin Guiteau: Psychiatry and Law in the Gilded Age* ((Univ. of Chicago Press, 1968)

Sterling, Christopher H. and Kittross, John Michael, *Stay Tuned: A History of American Broadcasting* (Lawrence Erlbaum Associates, 3rd ed., 2002)

Swanson, James L., *Manhunt: The 12-Day Chase for Lincoln's Killer* (Mariner Books, 2007)

Taylor, Tom, *Our American Cousin* (Independent Publication, May 29, 2020)

Wilber, Del Quentin, *Rawhide Down: The Near Assassination of Ronald Reagan* (Henry Holt & Co., 2011)

Yeats, William Butler, **The Second Coming** (1919)

Youngblood, Rufus W., *20 Years of the Secret Service: My Life with Five Presidents* (Fideli Publishing, Inc., 2nd ed., 2018)

Commission Reports

Preserving our Institutions: The First Report of the Continuity of Government Commission: The Congress (AEI-Brookings Institution, May 2003)

Preserving our Institutions: The Second Report of the Continuity of Government Commission: Presidential Succession (AEI-Brookings Institution, June 2009)

Continuity of Government: The Continuity of Congress, The Continuity of Government Commission (AEI, April 2022)

Continuity of Government: Presidential Succession, The Continuity of Government Commission (American Enterprise Institute, Dec. 2022)

Articles

Collins, Kaitlin & Gray, Noah, *Trump briefly taken to underground bunker during Friday's White House protest* (CNN, June 1, 2020)

Feerick, John D., *The Proposed Twenty-Fifth Amendment to the Constitution,* Fordham Law. Rev. 173, vol. 34, Issue 2 (1965)

Goldstein, Joel K, *Birch Bayh and the Twenty-Fifth Amendment: Lessons in Leadership,* vol. 89, Fordham Law Review, p. 50 (2020).

Goldstein, Joel K., *History of the Legislative Succession Provisions in the Presidential Succession Act of 1947*, vol. 91, Fordham Law Review, p. 13 (2022).

Murrill, Brandon J., *The Twenty-Fifth Amendment and Presidential Inability, Part 6: Final Approval and Implementation*, p. 2 (CRS Report LLSB11136 (Congressional Research Service, March 28, 2024).

National Emergency Powers (Congressional Research Service, Feb. 27, 2019).

Rambaran, Verdana, *At least 60 Secret Service members injured during George Floyd protests in D.C.* (Fox News, May 31, 2020)

Relyea, Harold C., *Martial Law and National Emergency*, CRS Report for Congress (Congressional Research Service, Jan. 7, 2005).

ENDNOTES

LINKS TO INTERNET SOURCES

i https://pjmedia.com/matt-margolis/2022/07/25/the-white-house-isnt-grooming-kamala-harris-for-the-presidency-n1615629

ii https://www.breitbart.com/clips/2022/07/23/desantis-kamala-harris-the-best-impeachment-25th-amendment-insurance-biden-could-have/

iii https://www.breitbart.com/clips/2021/07/23/fmr-wh-doc-gop-rep-jackson-biden-will-resign-or-face-25th-amendment-natl-security-issue/ (5:16)

iv https://www.livescience.com/61451-trump-cognitive-test-results.html

v https://www.carepatron.com/files/moca-test-example.pdf

vi https://slaynews.com/news/54-republicans-demand-joe-biden-take-cognitive-test-and-show-results-to-american-people/

vii https://www.wsj.com/articles/my-memory-is-fine-another-unforgettable-denial-of-reality-special-counsel-hur-848d9b74

viii https://www.breitbart.com/clips/2024/02/12/gop-rep-jackson-perfect-scenario-for-kamala-harris-to-become-president/ (8:06)

ix https://www.breitbart.com/politics/2024/02/08/sen-rick-scott-time-president-joe-bidens-cabinet-invoke-25th-amendment/

x https://www.breitbart.com/politics/2024/02/08/sen-rick-scott-time-president-joe-bidens-cabinet-invoke-25th-amendment/ (3:24)

xi https://www.nbcnews.com/politics/2024-election/bidens-age-fitness-top-list-voters-concerns-poll-finds-rcna137212

xii https://www.nbcnews.com/politics/2024-election/-nightmare-special-counsels-assessment-bidens-mental-fitness-triggers-rcna137975

xiii https://thehill.com/homenews/campaign/4202646-61-percent-support-age-cap-for-presidential-candidates-survey/

xiv https://www.foxnews.com/video/6346755729112

xv https://www.cnn.com/2024/02/12/media/super-bowl-lviii-ratings/index.html

xvi https://apnews.com/article/state-of-the-union-address-joe-biden-arts-and-entertainment-donald-trump-0b9a555067687c501e767bad48e0a6f5

xvii https://pinkerton.com/our-story/history

xviii https://www.nps.gov/foth/learn/historyculture/the-lincoln-conspirators.htm

xix https://www.thoughtco.com/presidential-salaries-through-the-years-3368133

xx https://www.battlefields.org/learn/primary-sources/abraham-lincolns-second-inaugural-address

xxi https://www.britannica.com/topic/yellow-journalism

xxii https://www.grunge.com/374198/a-look-at-the-assassination-attempts-against-harry-truman/

xxiii https://en.wikipedia.org/wiki/Manson_Family

xxiv https://www.imdb.com/title/tt0047749/

xxv https://www.famous-trials.com/johnhinckley

xxvi https://www.upi.com/Top_News/US/2016/07/27/Judge-orders-release-of-John-Hinckley-Jr-who-shot-Ronald-Reagan-in-1981/7471469629218/

xxvii https://pjmedia.com/news-and-politics/kevindowneyjr/2022/07/28/would-be-kavanaugh-assassin-was-shooting-for-three-justices-sources-confirm-n1616543

xxviii https://pjmedia.com/kevindowneyjr/2022/07/28/would-be-kavanaugh-assassin-was-shooting-for-three-justices-sources-confirm-n1616543

xxix https://thehill.com/homenews/senate/486007-schumer-warns-kavanaugh-and-gorsuch-they-will-pay-the-price/

xxx https://www.law.cornell.edu/constitution

xxxi https://en.wikipedia.org/wiki/List_of_vice_presidents_of_the_United_States

xxxii

https://en.wikipedia.org/wiki/List_of_United_States_Congr
esses

xxxiii

https://en.wikipedia.org/wiki/List_of_speakers_of_the_Uni
ted_States_House_of_Representatives

xxxiv

https://en.wikipedia.org/wiki/List_of_presidents_pro_temp
ore_of_the_United_States_Senate

xxxv https://www.law.cornell.edu/constitution

xxxvi https://www.law.cornell.edu/uscode/text/3/19

xxxvii https://usconstitution.net/const.html

xxxviii

https://constitution.congress.gov/constitution/amendment-
12/

xxxix https://www.jfklibrary.org/learn/about-jfk/jfk-in-
history/cuban-missile-crisis

xl https://www.poetryfoundation.org/poems/43290/the-
second-coming

xli https://www.deseret.com/2001/9/15/19606632/we-ll-
never-be-young-again

xlii https://www.law.cornell.edu/constitution/amendmentxx

xliii https://www.jfklibrary.org/learn/about-jfk/historic-
speeches/inaugural-address

xliv https://www.mayoclinic.org/diseases-conditions/addisons-disease/symptoms-causes/syc-20350293

xlv https://www.brainyquote.com/quotes/john_f_kennedy_114932

xlvi https://www.nytimes.com/1963/11/23/why-america-weeps-kennedy-victim-of-violent-streak-he-sought-to-curb-in-the-nation.html

xlvii https://constitution.congress.gov/constitution/amendment-25/

xlviii https://en.wikipedia.org/wiki/Watergate_complex%252525 25252525252523Watergate_Hotel_and_Office_Building

xlix https://en.wikipedia.org/wiki/United_States_Senate_Watergate_Committee

l https://www.britannica.com/biography/Spiro-Agnew

li https://en.wikipedia.org/wiki/Saturday_Night_Massacre

lii https://en.wikipedia.org/wiki/Yom_Kippur_War

liii https://en.wikipedia.org/wiki/1973_oil_crisis

liv https://www.defconlevel.com/defcon-levels.php

lv https://en.wikipedia.org/wiki/Battle_of_Waterloo

[lvi] https://supreme.justia.com/cases/federal/us/418/683/

[lvii] https://www.answers.com/Q/Why_didn't_Justice_Rehnquist_participate_in_the_US_v._Nixon_case

[lviii] https://www.law.cornell.edu/constitution-conan/article-2/section-4/the-nixon-impeachment-proceedings

[lix] https://www.ushistory.org/documents/constitution.htm

[lx] https://en.wikipedia.org/wiki/War_on_terror

[lxi] https://ir.lawnet.fordham.edu/cgi/viewcontent.cgi?article=1015&context=twentyfifth_amendment_executive_materials

[lxii] https://www.huffpost.com/entry/rod-rosenstein-donald-trump-25th-amendment_n_5ba53007e4b069d5f9d29afa

[lxiii] https://www.washingtonpost.com/outlook/2020/10/02/trump-covid-25th-amendment/

[lxiv] https://www.youtube.com/watch?v=DiFPGY5GwsM

[lxv] https://en.wikipedia.org/wiki/Second_impeachment_of_Donald_Trump

[lxvi] https://abcnews.go.com/Politics/president-donald-trump-acquitted/story?id=75853994

lxvii

https://www.usatoday.com/story/news/politics/2021/11/1
9/joe-biden-undergo-routine-annual-physical/8679730002/

lxviii https://www.wsj.com/articles/vice-president-kamala-
harris-ready-to-serve-president-joe-biden-d1b2041e

lxix

https://www.washingtonpost.com/history/2019/12/18/rep
ublic-if-you-can-keep-it-did-ben-franklin-really-say-
impeachment-days-favorite-quote/

lxx https://www.law.cornell.edu/uscode/text/18/3056

lxxi https://www.foxnews.com/video/6359828504112

lxxii https://hotair.com/david-strom/2024/08/06/thoughts-
on-the-secret-service-n3792735

lxxiii https://pjmedia.com/matt-margolis/2024/07/23/secret-
service-director-kimberly-cheatle-resigns-n4930976

lxxiv https://nypost.com/2024/07/22/us-news/kimberly-
cheatle-admits-trump-shooting-was-worst-secret-service-
blunder-in-decades-on-july-13th-we-failed/

lxxv https://www.breitbart.com/politics/2024/07/19/nine-
secret-service-failures-that-nearly-led-to-former-president-
donald-trump-being-assassinated/

lxxvi https://www.foxnews.com/us/officer-reported-man-
trump-rally-range-finder-30-mins-before-assassination-
attempt-source

lxxvii https://www.thedailybeast.com/even-trump-shooter-thomas-crooks-had-a-drone-why-didnt-the-secret-service

lxxviii https://pjmedia.com/matt-margolis/2024/07/20/we-have-yet-another-disturbing-update-on-the-trump-assassination-attempt-n4930892

lxxix https://www.foxnews.com/video/6359773591112

lxxx https://www.foxnews.com/us/pennsylvania-swat-officer-says-team-no-contact-secret-service-before-trump-rally-shooting

lxxxi https://cyberguy.com/news/this-drone-detection-technology-could-have-intercepted-assassins-drone-two-hours-before-trump-shooting/

lxxxii https://tile.loc.gov/storage-services/service/ll/llsl/llsl-c3/llsl-c3.pdf

lxxxiii

https://en.wikipedia.org/wiki/United_Airlines_Flight_93

lxxxiv

https://constitution.congress.gov/constitution/amendment-23/

lxxxv https://constitutioncenter.org/the-constitution/amendments/amendment-xxiv

lxxxvi

https://en.wikipedia.org/wiki/2020_United_States_redistricting_cycle

lxxxvii

https://en.wikipedia.org/wiki/United_States_presidential_line_of_succession

lxxxviii https://www.secretservice.gov/

lxxxix https://www.law.cornell.edu/uscode/text/40/6121

xc

https://www.americanrhetoric.com/speeches/alexandersolzhenitsynharvard.htm

Made in the USA
Middletown, DE
10 November 2024